HOW TO CHEAT AT COOKING

D0767552

Delia Smith is one of the most popular cookery experts writing today.

Justly famous for her *Evening Standard* and *Evening News* columns (syndicated world-wide) and for her numerous appearances on television – in *Family Fare*, *Look East*, *Multi-Coloured Swop Shop* and, above all, the phenomenally successful BBC TV series, *Delia Smith's Cookery Course* – she has a huge and devoted following.

On top of her television and newspaper journalism, she has delighted millions of cooks the world over with her many publications, including the classic paperbacks, FRUGAL FOOD, DELIA SMITH'S BOOK OF CAKES and THE *EVENING STANDARD* COOKBOOK – all available from Coronet.

**Also by the same author,
and available in Coronet Books:**

Frugal Food
The *Evening Standard* Cookbook

How to Cheat at Cooking

Delia Smith

Illustrated by Ivan Ripley

CORONET BOOKS
Hodder and Stoughton

Copyright © 1971 by Delia Smith

First published in Great Britain 1971 by
Ebury Press Ltd.

Coronet edition 1973
Eleventh impression 1980

Line drawings by Ivan Ripley

Printed and bound in Great Britain for
Hodder and Stoughton Paperbacks,
a division of Hodder and Stoughton Ltd.,
Mill Road, Dunton Green, Sevenoaks, Kent
(Editorial Office: 47 Bedford Square,
London, WC1 3DP), by
Hunt Barnard Printing Ltd.,
Aylesbury, Bucks.

ISBN 0 340 16876 5

CONTENTS

INTRODUCTION

If you're one of those dedicated cooks who's a keen early-morning mushroom gatherer and wouldn't dream of concocting a salad without using the 'just-picked' variety, then this book is not for you. The following pages are for those who like to eat and entertain, who want to cook, but simply don't have the will or the time to spend hours shopping, preparing or cooking. The recipes are aimed at helping you to use fresh and convenience foods to prepare meals reasonably quickly, and at the same time convince everyone that they're strictly *homemade*. Out-of-the-can cookery doesn't fool anyone – it's usually instantly recognisable. A can of diced corned beef added to a can of baked beans and topped with potato, for example, will always taste exactly what it is, no matter whether you call it *Cowboy Hash* or *Jiffy Bake*. Such transparent cheating is not for the *discerning* cheat for whom this book is intended.

The recipes that follow are of three distinct kinds (and each one is labelled with its appropriate code):

✳ COOK-AHEAD: these dishes can be prepared *and* cooked in advance – anything up to 24 hours before you need to serve them and reheated just before required.

✺ UP TO 30 MINS: these are recipes which make use of convenience foods (though not exclusively) and won't take you more than 30 minutes to prepare and cook.

✧ OVER 30 MINS: these will take rather longer to make, but are *not* complicated and will require no great feats of culinary expertise.

All the recipes, you'll find, take a lot less time than your guests will ever imagine, and, assuming you don't give the game away it won't be long, either, before you're an accomplished cheat. But before you embark on your career, you

should know that *the quantities given for canned ingredients
are approximate* – by necessity, because the quantities vary
from one brand to another. They do not, however, vary
by more than 1 oz. either way, and since the quantities are
primarily intended to indicate the size of the can, these
variations will in no way affect the quality of the recipe.

Also, if you can't buy the brands recommended in some
of the recipes, similar alternatives should do.

And, finally, before you start, you must learn the rules
of the game:

THE CHEAT'S CHARTER

1. *There are more important things in life than cooking.*
That is to say, cheats are people who enjoy eating but like
to spend the best part of their lives in places other than the
kitchen. They're not defeatists who hate to cook. They're
willing to have a go because they have to and, because they
have to, they like to make a good job of it without lots of
unnecessary bother. Cheats have given up reading cookery
books – instructions 'to continue in the usual way' send them
reaching for the tin-opener. For all they know Brown Roux
is a species of butterfly and Demiglace a half-portion of
ice-cream.

2. *If something tastes good, it is good.*
If it only took 20 minutes to make, so what? The flood
of cookery manuals, part-works and tele virtuosi seems to
have convinced us all that we need to be frightfully pains-
taking cooks. However, at the other end of the scale, cooking for the sake of speed alone – regardless of the end
product – is not part of the cheat's code of ethics. Cheats,
then, go for good flavoursome food and no fussing.

3. *There's no substitute for shopping.*
If you're not a good cook, then you've simply got to be an
extremely good shopper. Experienced cheats know where
the best bakers are; they always serve delicious crusty bread
and fresh creamy butter. They know where to get cakes
that pass for homemade. They have delicious, tempting fruit
bowls, they get to know all about unusual cheeses. They
know where to buy good coffee and which tea-bags are
best. All these things don't cost a minute's extra cooking
time.

4. *Never do yourself what you can get someone else to
do for you.*
Just think, there's your butcher with at least a-half-dozen

9

razor-sharp knives and a couple of lethal choppers just waiting to do all your boning, chopping, jointing and general preparing. The same goes for the fishmonger who'll happily clean, scale or fillet if you ask. Remember these men are experts. Your dedicated cook struggles with the step-by-step pictures in her technicolour cookbook; you sit and sun yourself in the garden (and if the tradesmen deliver as well, you might even get a tan).

5. *Exploit your supermarket.*
Now and then spend a little time just looking around the shelves. Think how much you miss hurrying around grabbing only the essentials. There are whole research teams dedicating their lives to helping you avoid cooking. Maybe they haven't got you right out of the kitchen as yet, but the results of their labour can certainly reduce the time you spend in it. A little tarting up by you of the tinned, packeted, frozen or dehydrated product will take care of your creative instincts and probably enable you to pass it off as something you created from scratch.

6. *Create an aura of good cooking in your home.*
Fill your kitchen with serious-looking accoutrements. Indifferent cooks always give themselves away with battered saucepans, and ill-fitting lids. Streamlined cheats, however, use non-stick frying pans, attractively coloured oven-to-table type casseroles, possibly even an automatic cooker. Also, have lots of intriguing jars for your herbs and spices. Shops that sell fashionable junk have delightful-looking bottles with that well-worn look (they'll look very phoney if they're choc-a-bloc full, by the way, so never quite fill them up). Bunches of dried herbs hanging around create a good impression, so does a branch of bay leaves. Of course, you must have plenty of top-drawer cook books placed in full view (needless to say keep *this one* well hidden!).

7. *Sell on sight.*
Meaning, the way you present food is half the battle won. Of course, we have all heard this before. Cookery books go on and on about it and head waiters perspire

over it. Going mad with presentation can be utterly vulgar – 'boats' and 'nests' and 'baskets' of any description are right out. So are tomato water-lilies, radish roses or any other horticultural effect. The way to 'sell' is with quiet confidence and modest good taste; and nothing flatters food more than a tasteful table ... which means taking trouble with details like glasses (classical-shaped, rather than off-licence tumblers) and colour schemes. A total, all-in-one scheme for tablecloth, napkins, candles and flowers can be most attractive; in summer choose all white, or cooler shades; in winter go for the warmer colours like sage-green or plum.

8. *Never apologise, never explain.*

Nothing makes one more uncomfortable than a hostess nervously making excuses before a meal or during it. Never, never explain your successes either. Cheats, after all, are not on strong ground here unless they lie in their teeth. So, if anyone asks you for a recipe, tell them you're one of those frightful cooks who never measures anything and you can't take on the responsibility of writing it all down.

9. *Plan ahead.*

Obviously anyone who hates to cook will spend as little time at it as possible – even people who claim to like it complain that mealtime follows mealtime and that there's no escaping for very long. One approach to this problem for cheats is to get a lot of it done at once. Provided you own a refrigerator you can, and would be well-advised to, bash off two or three cook-ahead meals at a time. Then use them as and when you need them during the week.

10. *Down with deep-freeze.*

Cheats at cooking never own deep-freezers; it's far too much sweat first getting things frozen and then un-freezing them again. The freezing compartment of your fridge, however, should always be as well-stocked as you can keep it. Ice-cream, for instance, should always be available (a couple of Bertorelli's specialities stored away, and you need never be short of a dessert). Good freezer standbys are frozen potted shrimps, prawns and plaice fillets; ratatouille (Findus) and baby onions in cream sauce (Birds Eye) – both can be poured over chops or steaks to give them an edge. Remember, when you do store things in the freezing compartment, make sure you follow the instructions on the packets: if the freezer's marked with one star, you can keep things in it for up to a week; two stars for up to a month; three stars up to three months. See Miscellaneous Tips and Hints for further information.

CHEATS KITCHEN

CHEAT'S EQUIPMENT

Among other things, the recipes in this book are intended to save you time and effort in the kitchen and to cover up, what should we say, a certain lack of dedication to the finer points of cooking. But without a few basic items of equipment no amount of can-opening or short-cutting is going to compensate for your waste of time. If you try to scrape new potatoes with a serrated bread knife, or strain a lumpy sauce through a tea strainer – it's going to take you twice as long. It always seems to be the people who have 'no time for cooking' who spend the most time over straightforward operations by trying to muddle through.

Don't get me wrong, though. I'm not the gadget type. All those miraculous 'labour-saving' devices require highly intricate washing and de-clogging (not to mention drying). So my advice is to stay clear of lady demonstrators in department stores. They make it look so easy, but you never see them washing up! None of the items I consider important for *your* kitchen are particularly glamorous, but they are quite indispensable.

We all know about those clever cooks who never measure anything and just throw in handfuls of this and that by instinct and everything turns out perfectly. But trying to measure ½ lb., of something by holding the guessed amount in one hand and ½ lb. of butter in the other is definitely not on. *Kitchen scales* take only seconds to give you an exact weight and are high up on my list of timesavers. Likewise, a *measuring jug* will save you hours trying to guess what a third of a pint looks like.

Blunt knives are what cause you to cut your fingers – a really *sharp knife* makes any cutting easy (nervous carvers please note). Apart from a multi-purpose small knife, you should also have at least two more of varying lengths and a *palette knife* for scraping bowls and sliding underneath things to lift them. The French carbonated steel knives sharpen easily and although there are many kinds of knife sharpener available, a proper *butcher's steel* is far the best (if you can't get the hang of it, pop into the butcher's when it's quiet, smile a lot and ask him if he wouldn't mind sharpening your knives, as you've noticed how well he does it).

Kitchen spoons are always important. It's essential to have a fairly large *ladle*, a *fish slice*, at least three or four *wooden spoons* (stirring things in saucepans with metal spoons will ruin your saucepans) and a large perforated *draining-spoon*. Holding a saucepan-lid slightly off and letting the hot water pour out is a highly unsatisfactory method of straining vegetables. First, you may burn your hands; secondly, you probably won't get all the water out and thirdly, half the vegetables may come out with it and into the bowl of dirty washing-up. So invest in a hard-wearing *metal collander* (not the plastic kind, which if left too near a heated stove, and this can happen, will melt). And have a fair-sized *sieve* hanging up somewhere where you can grab it quickly to extract lumps from sauces and gravies before anyone notices.

Chopping things on the draining-board will very swiftly ruin your knives, a wooden *chopping-board* won't. And for those things that need to be shredded quickly (apples, carrots, cucumbers etc.) a wooden *mandoline* will do it in no time at all. Apart from their hundreds of other uses *kitchen scissors* make jointing cooked chicken child's play. Use them for cutting cooked duck into quarters, too.

And as you'll see from a good many recipes in this book, you'd do well to invest in a *garlic crusher*, which is far the quickest way of mashing garlic to a pulp and extracting all the juice.

With lemons and oranges also playing an important part in the recipes, don't omit a *squeezer* from your armoury, nor a *zester*. This ingenious little invention takes off all the outer peel and essence of lemons or oranges in just a few moments. What's more, there's no waste unlike those graters which have to be soaked for hours to get all the peel out again. Of the standard types of grater, I've always found the *four-sided grater* with a handle to be the most effective and very easy to keep clean.

Finally, a *blender* or *liquidiser* is the one luxury item on this list, because it really does save so much time in making soups and sauces, chopping things and making breadcrumbs and so on, indefinitely. Expensive, yes, but it will pay for itself time and again. If you've got strong arms and can do without a rotary whisk or electric mixer (both of which do a pretty efficient job), a *balloon whisk* is a good all-rounder and beats egg whites better than anything else, since it gets the maximum amount of air in.

Now, provided you have a cooker, a set of saucepans, mixing-bowls, meat-tins etc., you can proceed to study the art of crafty cooking and convince everyone that you're a fully-fledged cordon bleu. But not without a *pepper-mill*, so that you can use freshly-milled pepper all the time you're cooking, and without which you're not going to fool anyone.

The Cheat's Store-cupboard

Every time you go out shopping, you must keep your eyes open for those hundreds of aids to short-cut cooking which appear almost daily in the shops. Supermarkets in particular (but also delicatessens and health-food stores) are good hunting-grounds, and an accomplished cheat will soon get to know how each firm can help her most: instant desserts, trifles and fruit salads, for instance, in Marks and Spencer's food departments (not to mention their ready-prepared vegetables, their high-quality pies, tarts and prepared meats, and instant chocolate sauce in a tube); in Sainsburys, their filleted herrings, their frozen stewpacks (that contain a whole mixture of stew-type vegetables including whole baby onions) and their Swiss breakfast mixture.

If you live a long way from town, or the shops aren't particularly enterprising in your area, remember that several London food stores do a mail order service for any item that will keep in the post (you'll find a short list with addresses on p. 158).

Once you've discovered your own sources of supply, then make sure you keep stocks well up at your end. For those embarking on a career of quick cooking, this is my list of basics which you should try and not run out of:

For sauces, soups etc, and starters	*Cans* of dried milk (for making up sauces), cream soups, tuna fish, sardines, crab or prawns, apple sauce, apple chutney, sauces (e.g. Bolognese), Spanish Rice (Libby's), Parmesan cheese (Kraft). *Packets* of instant sauce mix, various soups. *Jars* of mayonnaise (Hellman's), tartare sauce (Sainsbury's), mint sauce, redcurrant jelly (Wilkin & Son, Tiptree), horseradish sauce (Sainsbury's)
Stews, casseroles and main courses:	*Packets* of instant mashed potato, long grain rice (Uncle Ben's). *Cans* of tomatoes (small and large), (Britivic Spanish or Cirio Italian), minced beef (large), (Marks and Spencer), new potatoes (M & S or Sainsbury's), Swiss pâté (Le Parfait), carrots and chopped leaf spinach (Smedleys), mixed vegetables (Culina), pimentoes, ham (Marks and Spencer Danish), curry sauce, *Jars* of dehydrated onions (Mc-

Cormick's), dehydrated mixed vegetables (Bat-chelor's), green and red peppers (Batchelor's), instant beef stock and chicken stock (Knorr), Worcestershire sauce (Lea and Perrins).

Sweets, etc: *Cans* of instant custard, fruit pie fillings (Morton's), continental instant coffee, various dried fruits.
Packets of crumble topping (Viota), trifle sponge cakes, nibbed nuts, flaked almonds, coffee bags (Twinings, Tetley's or Marks and Spencer), tea bags (Brook Bond choicest or Tetleys).
Tube of instant chocolate sauce (Marks and Spencer).

Your cooking oil should be groundnut or olive oil. Use any make of wine vinegar, and always have an assortment of mustards. Try and keep a small selection of wine, spirits and liqueurs that don't find their way into the drinks cup-board: red/white wine, dry cider, sherry, brandy and liqueurs you most fancy.

Herbs and Spices

If you don't have much time for cooking, then you simply must have a few of the basic herbs and spices hanging around your kitchen. And, more important, you must familiarise yourself with the various ways and means of using them. *Don't* treat them like a junior chemistry set and try to be clever by throwing in a bit of this and a bit of that, making a devil's brew of the flavours. All the obvious cheats do that; real cooks use their spices carefully and subtly, and although we're cheating in this book we *are* trying to achieve results that compare favourably with the real thing. So please read this chapter carefully and learn how to use spices sensibly. And don't underestimate the advantage of having a few interesting-looking jars strategically placed about the kit-chen – so everyone will get the impression you're a deadly serious cook.

Herbs

Fresh parsley: first and foremost, always remember to grab a small bunch of fresh parsley every time you're in the greengrocer's. It's the most indispensable of all the herbs. It's rich in vitamin C, and not only does it add flavour but, as a garnish, it manages to jazz up the very dullest of dishes. Keep it on your kitchen windowsill, like flowers, with the stalks immersed in water. Then it's easy to snip off a few sprigs for garnishing anything that lacks a bit of colour. Think how a dish of bought sausage rolls can be made to look far more appetising arranged with sprigs of green parsley. Chopped, it can be sprinkled on almost anything savoury – salads, casseroles, soups. You name it, parsley will improve it.

Dried parsley: careful with this one. A tiny bit is ok, but too much and it looks and tastes like dried tea leaves.

Rosemary: is a very aromatic herb, so don't go mad with it. Dried, the spiky needles crush easily pressed on a chopping board with the back of a tablespoon. The flavour of rosemary does wonders for pork, lamb and veal. Crush it, sprinkle it over chops or put a little underneath the joint in a roasting tin. Try some added to beef casseroles, and sprinkle some over fried potatoes the way Italians do.

Thyme: a little dried thyme is excellent rubbed into pork chops before roasting, and when imported tomatoes are particularly flavourless, halve them and sprinkle them with a mixture of breadcrumbs (from a packet), olive oil, thyme and crushed garlic. Put a ½ teaspoon on each tomato half and bake in the oven till the crumbs are browned.

Sage: again, is good with pork. Rub some into chops and joints before roasting. Sprinkle a little on pork sausage before grilling or on to grated cheese for cheese on toast.

Bay leaves: a branch of bay leaves hung up somewhere in the kitchen will look like you're really professsional. Bay leaves should be added to soups, stews, fish; and they do a lot for some packet sauces. A bay leaf added to a can of rice pudding heated gently for 15 minutes gives it a taste that's slightly out of the ordinary.

Chives: belong to the onion family and are one of my favourites. They are sometimes difficult to get fresh, but if you can find potted ones, provided you water them and snip them often, they do go on for some time. If you can't get hold of fresh chives, the freeze-dried variety is fine. Add them to all tinned or packet creamy soups. Mix them with cream or butter to melt into jacket potatoes. and sprinkle them over fresh or canned buttered new potatoes.

Fresh mint: when it's in season, try not to be without it. It keeps very well sprinkled with a little water in a poly-thene bag. Freshly-chopped, its aroma is like a tonic. Fresh mint sauce really is nicer than the bottled stuff – and try adding fresh chopped spring onions as well. Fruit salad, orange and grapefruit sprinkled with chopped mint makes a good appetiser. Pea soups are all the better for it, and buttered new potatoes (canned ones like a generous amount sprinkled over). Grilled lamb chops are delicious with mint butter. Use 1 tablespoon of fresh chopped mint to 1 oz. of butter and add pepper and salt.

Dried mint: is like dried parsley. Be very careful with it and use sparingly.

Mixed herbs: are useful for a great number of recipes. A level teaspoonful with a little freshly-chopped parsley makes a plain omelette a bit more special. Add it to canned minced steak or canned stewing beef. If you're entertaining serve a hot herb loaf: mix 1 tablespoon of mixed herbs with ¼ lb. of softened butter. Cut a medium-sized French loaf almost into slices (but leaving the base whole). Put a dab of herb butter in between the slices, wrap in foil and bake in a moderate oven for 15 minutes. The loaf will be hot and buttery and flavoured with herbs.

Basil: if you like Italian food, you can't afford to be without some dried basil. *All* tinned Italian tomato-based sauces are greatly improved with a pinch or two of basil. Add it to tomato soups, tinned tomatoes, or sprinkle it over fresh tomato and onion salad, rice salads or any green salads.

Garlic: well, one man's meat, of course ... so it's really up to you how much you use (or whether you use it at all). If you like it crush it and add it to salad dressings, mayonnaise, and put 1 or 2 cloves under joints of lamb or pork before roasting. Garlic bread is made in the same way as herb bread (p. 21) substituting 2 cloves of garlic for the herbs.

Tarragon: dried, it's delicious crumbled and added to cream of chicken soup (1 level teaspoon) and cream chicken casseroles (see page 78). Tarragon goes very well into butter sauces for fish and meat, and if you're in a hurry simply make tarragon butter: 1 oz. of butter and 1 level teaspoon of tarragon per person, and let it melt over lamb chops, steaks and any fish – even fish fingers. It's also nice added to salads.

Spices

Nutmeg: my most important spice. The French almost totally ignore it, but the Italians are devoted to it and it was used extensively in Eighteenth Century English cooking. Always buy *whole* nutmegs – once ground they lose a lot of their flavour. Most good kitchen shops stock a small nutmeg grater with a little container to keep the nuts in. Grate into canned rice puddings, cream of onion or celery soups. Nutmeg does wonders, too, for packet sauces. Try it with onion sauce, white sauce or cheese sauce. Add it to milk puddings, or sprinkle about a quarter of a nutmeg grated over cauliflower or into canned red cabbage.

Whole cloves: try adding 6 whole cloves to a packet bread sauce and let them infuse in it for 15 minutes. Baked apples, apple tarts and crumbles are all improved with the delicate aroma of cloves. They're also good when added to rice for curries (see p. 122).

Ground cinnamon: mixed with soft brown sugar can be sprinkled over pancakes, bought treacle tarts and fruit crumbles. I suggest you might like a teaspoon added to canned minced steak with a dollop of tomato purée.

Dried ginger: a couple of pinches added to rhubarb (tinned or fresh), rhubarb crumble or rhubarb fool will bring out the flavour nicely. It's also used a great deal in curries, so why not add a little to canned curries and curry sauce. Try the recipe for Pork with Honey and Ginger (see p. 101).

Paprika: comes from sweet red peppers. The Hungarian variety is supposed to be the best and goes to make a very good beef goulash (see p. 105). Use it, too, for garnishing. A lot of pale uninteresting food can be livened up with a judicious sprinkling of paprika (cauliflower cheese, say, or macaroni cheese or cheese on toast).

Curry spices: cheating at cooking obviously can't involve long drawn-out curry making sessions. However, always have *curry powder* handy for adding to other things like soups, mayonnaise, eggs, vegetables and salads. *Ground turmeric* is an economical way of colouring rice for curries and gives it a distinctive flavour.

Last but not least, you must stock *whole black peppercorns* if you're going to convince anyone you're good at cooking.

For their entertainment

Cheats can often give just as good dinner parties as real, hard-working cooks with half the effort. Our recipes need no last-minute flapping over, our soufflés never fall flat — because we never make soufflés. What we may have lacked in the kitchen, we can make up for in the dining-room, getting everything quietly organised, making ourselves look as delicious as possible, even refraining from cutting short a rivetting conversation by quick sprints into the kitchen.

We never bore our guests with running commentaries and constant apologies as to why this or that went wrong. Well, it goes without saying that if you say the shrimp pâté isn't quite right, you may be sure everyone will take your word for it. If, on the other hand, you admit how particularly pleased you are with the shrimp pâté, of course everyone's going to think it's frightfully special. You needn't overdo it, but a little suggestion goes a long way.

But the most confident of cheats will go adrift if the setting for their dinner party is sloppy. If you're well-off you couldn't do better than use a white damask tablecloth with absolutely everything in solid silver and pure cut crystal glasses. But then you'd probably have a cook, too. Poorer entertainers can achieve impressive results by cultivating the 'total' look. Choose a plain tablecloth in a pleasant colour, then buy flowers, napkins and candles to match exactly. Yes, I did say flowers but if they're hard to get hold of fresh or are particularly expensive, most of those kitchen/gift shops sell tiny artificial ones that look good cut short and can be used as a centrepiece for the table. And don't be tempted to skimp on the candles – they'll flatter the room, you and your food.

BEFORE DINNER

A little selectivity about the drinks you're going to offer before the meal is important because they set the style for the evening. There's no need to take in a large range of bottles – that's a costly indulgence and as often as not you'll find your guests will all plump for the same and clean you out of it. Food-and-wine experts seldom drink spirits before dinner. Don't ask 'what'll you have?' either and then have to apologise for not having gin or vodka. Fortified wines are cheaper and you might do well to choose just one for an evening.

If you decide to have *sherry*, then the drier the better (although a medium sherry is a safer bet and satisfies a greater number). Recommend them to have a little ice in it – delicious and quite within the rules. If you're using a decanter, make sure you buy an acceptable Spanish variety, unless you want people to think you're doing a cover-up job for an inferior brand.

Vermouth is a pretty safe bet. I'd be surprised if at least one guest didn't ask 'what is it?' so choose an example that will give you the chance to drop the name of your wine-merchant (don't say off-licence). Chambery, for instance is very popular with gourmets – chill it and serve it with finely pared slivers of lemon peel.

It's expensive but *Campari* goes a long way and makes a

delightful aperitif for warm summer evenings. Chill it and serve it long with lots of ice and soda. Don't always rely on the ubiquitous lemon – a slice of orange goes equally well, it not better, with this.

There are plenty of other options open to you – a dry martini cocktail, a sparkling wine, even champagne if you're feeling rich – but a word of caution from bitter experience: I'd steer clear of cocktails, if I were you. The dedicated cocktail addict is so particular you may not get it right, and to cater for indifferent cocktail drinkers will mean you've gone to a lot of trouble for nothing.

AT DINNER

I'm not suggesting you must have a 108-piece dinner-service to offset your food-offerings, but never underestimate the touch of authenticity that an appropriate serving-dish can give. Canned and packet soups will most certainly taste better to your guests if you ladle them out of an attractive soup tureen. Fish starters can be enormously enhanced by being served in deep scallop shells (a good fishmonger should be able to get hold of some for you). Stews and casseroles obviously need to be served from a very French-looking cooking-pot, and wherever it's practicable try and arrange your main course with an attractive garnish on large serving dishes, and serve out somewhere at the side of the dining-tables (this applies especially to sauce-covered concoctions). This gives your guests an appetising eyeful of your efforts before they tuck in.

WINES

You won't go far wrong if you stick to the generally-accepted rule: where the flesh is white, the wine is white (with the corollary that red wine should be drunk with red meat). But that is only a starting-point; more important perhaps is to try and match flavours. Roast beef, for example, is perfectly partnered by a rich, full-bodied red Burgundy such as Gevrey Chambertin, whereas a lighter wine such as St. Emilion, which is a red Bordeaux, would be a better partner for lamb. White meats harmonise well with a light and dry Pouilly Fuissé and sea food with a light, fresh and young Muscadet. In other words, full wines with highly flavoured foods and light wines for more delicate dishes. With some foods, wine is to be avoided altogether: curries and highly-spiced food, cream soups, cocktail sauces, egg dishes and chocolate.

If you want to serve a wine to suit each course, once again there are some basic rules which, once you have tried them, will prove to be quite logical. They are: white before red, dry before sweet, light before full, young before old. These are based on the assumption that a meal should progress from less interesting wines to those with more flavour and complexity. So, a dry wine is correctly served with a first course, but would be disappointing after the greater richness of a red wine. Sweet white dessert wines are, of course, the exception and should always be served at the end of a meal. If you want to take the easy way out, though, you can serve champagne throughout the meal – a non-vintage is quite adequate. But remember that champagne is after all a light white wine varying in degrees of dryness, and therefore will not go with all foods.

The ideal shopping-place for the wine beginner is a wine supermarket, where you can study the range at leisure and take advantage of numerous cut-price offers. Wines offering best value for money are without doubt the *branded* wines which will also prevent you from making expensive mistakes at the start. Such brands might be Don Cortez Spanish wines (which have five in their range) or Nicolas French vin ordinaire (which have four). But if you want to keep away from the branded wine image, there are wines on most price-lists for under £1 a bottle. These are known as *generic* wines, and appear on the wine-list usually as non-vintage and under the collective name for an area: Bordeaux Rouge, St Emilion, Macon Rouge etc.

With anything more ambitious, you are best advised to consult a wine-merchant, such as Victoria Wine-Tylers in your high street or (if you want to tell your guests you share the same wine-merchant as the late Sir Winston Churchill) Hatch, Mansfield and Co., who operate on a direct sales basis to the public and – if you buy by the case, which can be mixed – will deliver to you free anywhere in the country. Finally, you won't have to look far in the papers and magazines nowadays to find special wine offers, which again means buying in bulk but will save you time and money.

Wine never really goes well with soup; so if you're starting with soup, don't pour until the main course. At the same time, if your guests are still drinking red wine after the main course why not serve the cheese *before* the dessert? Cheese has a special place in the cheat's repertoire – if only because, if served with style, you can get away without producing a dessert at all. A fine English Stilton, a bottle of vintage port (if you can afford one) and grapes (in two colours) make a grand finale to a meal, and you haven't had to cook a thing! Guests can be easily impressed and intrigued by your unusual selection of cheese (experiment yourself with the stock of your local delicatessen, but make certain you get to know the history of the ones you like because you're certain to be asked). Bear in mind that, on the whole, the British are pretty timid about experimenting with cheese – but here is a selection which should cater for the widest range of palates: *Stilton* (blue-veined English cheese), *Caerphilly* (a creamy, crumbly English cheese), *Austrian smoked* (smooth, smokey cheese sometimes with small bits of ham in it), *St Paulin* (French, creamy and fairly pungent), *Brie* (another creamy French cheese which should be running nicely), *Bresse Bleu* (an excellent French blue cheese), *Bel Paese* (creamy, mild and Italian), *Dolce latte* (a creamy, blue Italian variety) and *Boursin with pepper* (cream cheese with black pepper). All these are generally available from good grocers and delicatessens.

With your cheeses serve a selection of biscuits – Digestive, high-bake, water-biscuits or Bath Olivers (the poshest of all; serve them from their own classy tin so no one's in the least doubt as to what they are). You might also consider serving some celery, if you have any weight-watchers at the table. If you intend to finish up with a bowl of fruit, do polish each fruit with a bit of kitchen paper. It takes a few seconds, I know, but it makes them irresistible.

AFTER DINNER

The bottomless coffeepot can be a real sweat if you're the type who insists on an elaborate filtering or percolating performance. But provided you've got an (almost) bottomless pot, you can be pretty sure of extracting, if not a standing ovation, then a murmur of approval from:

(1) using (Lyons) fresh-ground, making it as you would make a cup of tea, and straining;

(2) boiling up coffee-bags in a saucepan with the right amount of water and serving directly – better than letting them stew;

(3) serving strong continental instant coffee with a topping of single cream.

No one will know you didn't actually roast and grind it yourself. If the meal hasn't been too rich and filling, you might for a special occasion like to serve Gaelic coffee. The easy way to make this is to heat up 4 measures of whisky, pour them into 4 glasses, stir in hot and strong continental coffee, add sugar and top with whipped cream (which will settle beautifully over the top and look quite authentic. After-dinner mints and dessert chocolates are fine, but don't get the obvious ones – here are so many unusual ones to choose from, raisins and rum, chocolate ginger, mint crisps and so on.

List of Recipes

SOUPS

This chapter is, with no apologies, an exercise in disguising. The one thing any cheat has to come to terms with straight away is the fact that the majority of packet and canned soups on their own taste like packet and canned soups. And more than that, the better a canned soup is, the more widely it will be used and the quicker your family and guests will recognise it.

Now your truly dedicated soup-maker spends hours in the kitchen with bones, stockpots, endless simmerings and strainings. And, of course, the result is invariably excellent. What we cheats have to do is get as good a result as they do with the minimum of effort. The simple fact for us to grasp, then, is that *somebody has already done all this hard work for us* when we use cans and packets. We come into our own by making *their* efforts taste like homemade soup. In other words we go straight to the creative part.

The accomplished cheat is not afraid of experimenting. He or she will, for instance, come to learn what soups can

✳ Cook-ahead   ✽ Up to 30 mins   ◊ Over 30 mins

combine together, what can be added to the basic varieties to make them different and to effect the desired transformation. But, clearly, he or she will not be totally indiscriminate: real success only comes through paying due attention to complementary combinations of flavour. Two delicate flavours such as asparagus and celery would simply cancel each other out. The recipes in this section will give you a guide as to what *is* possible.

But first a few general principles on the art of tarting-up, the most important of which are ADDING, GARNISHING, BLENDING and PRESENTATION.

ADDING:
Used with discretion, there are certain basic cheating ingredients which will cover most eventualities.

White wine, in general, may be added with great effect to fish soups. Always use a dry white wine (for instance an inexpensive Chablis) and if you're a bit hard up at the time try a dry cider. But don't be fobbed off at the off-licence with an ordinary flagon of cider, which will be semi-sweet.

Red wine will help to give a distinctive flavour to soups like tomato, minestrone and kidney. Once again only use a dry variety (preferably a good cheap Burgundy).

Sherry. Most clear soups will get a kick out of a couple of tablespoonfuls. So will Oxtail, game and thick fish soups such as tinned crab and lobster. Use a dry sherry and, ideally, a Spanish variety.

Brandy is strictly for the flamboyant cheats. Heat half a ladleful of brandy, set light to it and pour it flaming into bowls of tinned lobster or crab soup.

Cream, as you would expect, goes admirably into any cream soup. For a really creamy effect, try heating a can of condensed soup with a cup of milk, then at the last minute stir in ¼ pint of single cream. Let it heat without boiling. This is particularly good with condensed asparagus, celery and green pea soups.

Soured cream is sensational whisked into a tine of condensed tomato soup with ¼ pint of milk, then chilled thoroughly.

GARNISHING:

Parsley, of course, is the great soup standby, fulfilling the two important functions of a good garnish – adding a subtle extra taste, and providing some colour interest.

Freshly-chopped mint is great for all packet or tinned pea soups, but beware of using dried mint as it can resemble tea leaves if you're not careful. Try it, too, with cold cucumber soup.

Fresh chives are increasing in popularity and are now available in many good greengrocers in the summer months. Chop them with scissors and add them to almost any soup but especially to leek, onion and potato soups. Freeze-dried are a perfectly good substitute.

Croûtons (little squares of bread fried crisp in oil or dripping, sometimes flavoured with garlic) make any soup look as if you've *tried*.

Cream and soured cream, as a garnish. Put a dollop into the centre of a bowl of soup before serving and let your guests stir it in themselves. Again, suitable for all cream soups.

BLENDING:

Quite honestly, a liquidiser is the keystone of cheating with soups. If used only for soups it would earn its keep. It gives them a wonderful texture, and breaking vegetables down to a pulp makes extra thickening unnecessary. Cheats are often caught out by the tell-tale dehydrated texture of packet vegetable soups; liquidising prevents this from happening. Once you've followed the recipes in this chapter, you and your liquidiser will think of a thousand good ideas of your own. If you haven't got a liquidiser, give up cheating on soups now, because sieving takes hours.

PRESENTATION:

Finally, don't forget to serve your soups with good, fresh crusty bread and creamy butter. Better still, hot garlic or herb bread will really give you an edge (see pages 21 and 22). Remember this is the beginning of the meal and the atmosphere you create is most important. If you succeed at this stage, the odds are that the rest of the meal will be a success. Invest in a nice-looking soup tureen. And perhaps it goes without saying but a soup-bowl served on a plate is better than a soup-bowl plonked straight on to the table.

❊❊ Asparagus soup   (serves 4)

2 15 oz. cans of Asparagus soup, (Heinz)
1 10½ oz. can of All Green Asparagus tips, drained

A knob of fresh butter
3 tablespoons of double cream
Freshly-milled black pepper

Heat the soup along with the drained asparagus tips, and just before serving add a knob of butter and the cream and stir. Let it all melt and season with freshly-milled pepper before serving.

❊❊ Carrot and Potato soup   (serves 4)

1 15 oz. can of carrots
1 10 oz. can of new potatoes
1 10½ oz. can Concentrated Consommé (Campbell's)

1 tablespoon double cream
A knob of butter
Freshly-milled black pepper

Drain half the liquid from the can of carrots, then blend them into a purée in the liquidiser. Empty into a large saucepan. Repeat exactly with the can of potatoes. Now pour the consommé over the potatoes and carrots and heat gently, stirring with a wooden spoon to mix everything evenly. Just before serving add the cream, butter and freshly-milled black pepper.

❊ Consommé   (serves 2 – double for 4)

1 15 oz. can of Consommé (Baxters pheasant is a good one)
2 tablespoons of dry sherry
Freshly-milled black pepper

2 slices of stale bread
1 clove of garlic, crushed
A little dripping
1 tablespoon of parsley, fresh chopped

Gently heat the consommé with the sherry and season with freshly-milled black pepper. While that's going on, cut a couple of slices of stale bread. Remove the crusts and cut them into small cubes. Fry them in hot dripping or bacon fat to which you have added the crushed garlic. When they are hard and crisp and golden brown, drain them on some kitchen paper and serve the soup with the fried bread cubes sprinkled over and some freshly-chopped parsley.

✻ Celery soup   (serves 2 – double for 4)

2 sticks of celery, chopped small	½ pint of milk
1 oz. of butter	2 tablespoons of single cream
1 10½ oz. Condensed Cream of Celery soup (Campbell's)	A little fresh nutmeg, grated
	Freshly-milled black pepper

Melt some butter in a saucepan and gently cook the celery in it for about 10 minutes or until it's soft. At this stage your kitchen will have a sensational aroma drifting from it! Now simply pour in the soup and the milk, stir it a bit and heat it through. Add the cream, the nutmeg and the pepper – and it's ready.

✻ Thick Cheese and   (serves 2 – double for 4)
Onion Soup

1 packet of Thick Devon Onion soup (Batchelor's)	2 oz. of grated Cheddar cheese
A pinch of ground cloves	A knob of butter
A few gratings of whole nutmeg	Freshly-milled black pepper
	Hot buttered toast

Follow the instructions on the back of the packet. When the soup is cooked add the spices, stir in the cheese and butter to melt, and then the pepper. Serve with some hot buttered toast.

✺ French Onion Soup   (serves 4)

1 large Spanish onion, finely chopped
1 oz. of butter
2 10½ oz. cans of Condensed Onion soup (Campbell's)
¼ pint of water
¼ pint of dry white wine, or

¼ pint of dry cider
Freshly-milled black pepper
4 slices of French bread
3 oz. of Emmenthal cheese, grated
Some grated Parmesan

Pre-heat oven to 450°F (mark 8)

Gently cook the onion in the butter till it's soft for about 10–15 minutes. Now heat up the onion soup together with the water and the dry white wine. Add the onion you've softened and the black pepper, then toast the bread. Now pour into 4 heat proof bowls first the soup, then the bread, which should float on top. Sprinkle the Emmenthal cheese generously all over each piece then place the bread on the top shelf of the oven for about 10 minutes, till the cheese is melted and gooey. Now sprinkle on a tiny bit of Parmesan and serve immediately.

◊ Greek Lemon Soup   (serves 4)

2 15 oz. cans of Cream of Chicken soup (Heinz)
2 eggs, separated

Juice of 2 lemons
Grated rind of 1 lemon
Freshly-milled black pepper

Pour the soup into a saucepan and bring to simmering point. In a bowl, beat the egg yolks and slowly add the lemon juice and grated rind until well blended. Now add about half a ladleful of hot soup to the egg mixture and stir well. Add another ladleful and stir well again. Then pour the whole lot back into the hot soup, stirring continuously with the heat very low. Whisk the egg whites till they form soft peaks. Stir them into the soup, add a little pepper and let the soup stand for 3 minutes before serving.

Herb Soup

(serves 4)

- 2 pints of chicken stock (Knorr instant)
- 2 tablespoons of tomato purée
- 1 level teaspoon of thyme
- 1 level teaspoon of mixed herbs
- 1 level teaspoon of dried basil
- ½ small lettuce, shredded
- 1 bunch of spring onions, chopped small
- Salt and freshly-milled pepper

Put the chicken stock, tomato purée, herbs, lettuce, spring onions and seasoning into a saucepan and stir well. Bring to simmering point and simmer for 25 minutes. Taste to check seasoning before serving. A couple of handfuls of garlic croûtons go well with this (see recipe for Consommé p. 34).

❋ Italian Bean and Pasta Soup

(serves 4)

- 2 15½ oz. cans of Tomato soup (Heinz)
- 1 15 oz. can of Fagioli Italian White Beans (or if you can't get them, 1 14 oz. can of butter beans)
- 1 clove of garlic, crushed
- 1 level teaspoon of dried basil
- 1 heaped teaspoon of concentrated tomato purée
- 2 oz. of Macaroni (Quaker Quick)
- Grated Parmesan cheese
- Freshly-milled black pepper

Put the tomato soup into a large saucepan with the drained beans. Gently bring it to simmering point, then add the tomato purée, garlic and basil. Grab a wooden spoon and give the soup a good stir. Then throw in the macaroni, and let it all simmer for 11 minutes. Stir in a little grated Parmesan cheese, season with pepper, then serve with a bowl of Parmesan to sprinkle over.

❋ Leek and Potato Soup

(serves 4)

- 1 packet of Leek soup (Knorr)
- 1 15½ oz. can of Cottage Potato soup (Crosse and Blackwell)
- 1 tablespoon of chives, freeze-dried
- Freshly-milled black pepper
- 2 tablespoons of single cream
- ½ oz. of fresh unsalted butter
- 1 tablespoon of fresh parsley, chopped

Make the leek soup according to the directions on the packet, then add the canned soup and the chives and some pepper. Bring to simmering point, then turn the heat down very low. Add the cream and butter and stir in to melt. Serve with fresh-chopped parsley spinkled over.

✳ Quick Minestrone   (serves 6)

1 packet of Minestrone soup (Knorr)
1 level teaspoon of concentrated tomato purée
1 large clove of garlic, crushed
1 15½ oz. can of Tomato soup (Heinz)
Grated Parmesan cheese

1 can of Nocki (noodles in tomato sauce) (Crosse and Blackwell)
1 8 oz. can of butter beans, drained
1 level teaspoon of dried basil
Freshly-milled black pepper

First make-up the minestrone adding the tomato purée and the garlic. Let it simmer for around 20 minutes, or for however long the packet tells you to, then add the tomato soup and the Nocki. Take a wooden spoon and do a bit of continuous stirring till it all looks evenly blended, then again bring it to simmering point. Lastly, add the butter beans, the basil and a little grated Parmesan. Season with freshly-milled black pepper, then serve with lots more Parmesan sprinkled over.

✳ Shrimp Soup   (serves 2)

1 15½ oz. can of Cream of Mushroom soup (Heinz)
¼ pint of dry white wine, Sherry, or dry cider
2 tablespoons of double cream

2 2 oz. portions of Potted Shrimps (Young's)
2 pinches of powdered mace
Freshly-milled black pepper

Pour the soup into a saucepan and add the wine (or sherry or cider – whichever you have on hand) and potted shrimps. Stir in the cream and season with mace and pepper. Bring to simmering point and serve.

❋ Vegetable Potage   *(serves 4)*

2 packets of White Onion
  soup (Knorr)
2 tablespoons of single cream

1 14 oz. can of Mixed Vegetables, drained (Culina)
Freshly-milled black pepper

Make up the onion soup mix according to the instructions
on the packet, but watch it carefully -- this particular soup
has a habit of boiling over and finding its way into the most
unreachable corners of the stove! When the soup is ready,
add the drained vegetables, allow them to heat through, then
serve with the cream and pepper stirred in at the last minute.

❋ Cream of Vegetable Soup   *(serves 4)*

1 lb. of potatoes, peeled and
  diced
3 medium-sized carrots, peeled
  and sliced
1 large onion, peeled and
  chopped
2 leeks

2 oz. butter
1½ chicken stock cubes
1½ pints of boiling water
½ pint of milk
1 tablespoon of freshly
  chopped parsley
Salt and freshly-milled pepper

Trim the leeks, leaving about 1 inch of the green part.
Split them lengthwise, wash them thoroughly and slice them
finely into a bowl. Now melt the butter in a large saucepan
and empty into it the leeks, potatoes, carrots and onions,
stirring for a few minutes to nicely coat the vegetables.
Season well with the salt and pepper, put on the lid and let
them 'sweat' for about 10 minutes. Make up the stock,
dissolving the cubes in water. Pour it on to the vegetables
with the milk, and when it begins to simmer, replace the
lid and allow it to simmer for about 25 minutes on a low
heat. Then pour the soup into the goblet of your liquidiser
and blend for a few minutes until smooth. If necessary,
reheat briefly before serving.

COLD SOUPS

✳ Avocado Soup   *(serves 3 – double for 6)*

1 large avocado pear
1 clove of garlic
1 dessertspoon of lemon juice
½ pint of cold chicken stock
(made with a cube)

Salt and freshly-milled black
pepper
1 5 fl. oz. carton of soured
cream

Halve the avocado, remove the stone and scoop out all the flesh (taking great care to scrape out all the green part next to the skin). Chop the flesh roughly and then put it into the goblet of the liquidiser with the garlic, lemon juice, half the chicken stock and some salt and pepper. Blend on a high speed for about 15 seconds, then empty the contents into a soup tureen or bowl. Stir in the soured cream and the rest of the stock using a whisk to get it all blended evenly. Cover and chill thoroughly. Serve with cubes of ice.

Eat this soup on the day you make it. If it's kept too long it tends to discolour.

✳ Chilled Cucumber Soup   *(serves 4)*
with Mint

1½ medium-sized cucumbers
2 oz. butter
1 medium-sized potato,
chopped small
1 medium onion, chopped
small
Salt and freshly-milled pepper

1½ pints of chicken stock,
made with a cube
2 tablespoons of milk
2 tablespoons of double cream
2 tablespoons of mint, finely
chopped

First peel the cucumbers, keeping a quarter of one for later and chopping the rest into ¼-inch slices. Melt the butter in a saucepan, add the cucumber slices, potato and onion then put on the lid and let it cook gently for around 10 minutes. Give it all a good stir, add the stock, salt and pepper and milk and let it simmer with the lid on for about 25 minutes. When it's cooked, blend till smooth in a liquidiser. Taste to check the seasoning, pour the soup into a bowl to cool, cover with foil and chill thoroughly in the refrigerator.

Before serving stir in the cream, chop the remaining cucumber into small cubes and sprinkle them into the soup with the mint. Serve with an ice-cube in each soup bowl.

✳ Blender Gazpacho *(serves 4)*

1 14 oz. tin of tomatoes, chilled
1 19 fl. oz. tin of tomato juice, chilled
3 tablespoons of olive oil
3 tablespoons of wine vinegar
1 clove of garlic, crushed

½ green pepper, chopped
½ teaspoon of salt
½ small cucumber, grated
1 smallish onion, chopped very fine
6 cubes of ice

Put the tomatoes, the tomato juice, the olive oil, the wine vinegar, the garlic, half the green pepper and the salt into the liquidiser and blend for a few seconds. Pour out into a bowl and add the cucumber, the onion, and the remaining green pepper together with the ice-cubes. Stir the ice round until the mixture is very cold. Serve, giving everyone an ice-cube.

✳ Iced Watercress Soup *(serves 2 – double for 4)*

1 15½ oz. can of Cottage Potato soup (Crosse & Blackwell's)
1 bunch of watercress

Salt and freshly-milled black pepper
2 tablespoons of double cream

Empty the contents of the can of soup into the liquidiser and blend till smooth. Cut off all the leafy tops of the watercress with some scissors, add them to the soup in the liquidiser and switch on for a few seconds only till the leaves are chopped. Pour the soup into a tureen or bowl, season with salt and pepper then stir in the cream. Cover and chill thoroughly in the refrigerator. Serve with an ice-cube in each bowl.

NOTES

List of Recipes

STARTERS

Luckily there are now plenty of starters and appetisers that can be bought and served with no effort at all. These are all fine up to a point, but you can't fool anyone with them. I mean, people just don't smoke salmon nowadays. However, if you simply don't have the time for anything else, make sure you buy everything in first-class condition and be as tasteful as possible with the garnishings. Many delicatessens don't have a very quick turnover, so watch out for stale-looking pâtés, meats and fish. Try and sort out a really reliable shop for yourself (and if they're nice, they'll probably let you taste the various sausages and pâtés, so you don't waste money on things you're not going to like). Here are a few tips for serving instant starters — not forgetting that an interesting wine served with them will help a lot.

❋ *Duck Pâté:* serve on crisp green lettuce leaves, with a thin slice of orange twisted, and hot buttered toast.

❋ Cook-ahead   ❀ Up to 30 mins   ✣ Over 30 mins

❊ *Liver Pâté:* serve with thinly sliced dill cucumbers, shiny black olives and sprigs of watercress, together with croûtons (see p. 33).

❊ *Salami:* goes well with Italian pickled pimientoes or ordinary mixed pickles. Serve with fresh, hot crusty bread.

❊ *Smoked salmon:* serve it spread out on large plates with lemon quarters. Have ground cayenne pepper and a pepper mill on the table. Thinly sliced brown bread and butter is a must.

❊ *Smoked trout:* serve these on crisp lettuce leaves with lemon quarters and creamed horseradish to hand around. Again, thinly sliced brown bread and butter is good with it.

❊ *Potted shrimps:* serve with bunches of fresh watercress or mustard and cress with lemon quarters and brown bread and butter.

❊ *Frozen asparagus:* cook according to the instructions and serve with a jug of melted butter to pour over – or chill and serve cold with vinaigrette dressing or mayonnaise.

❊ *Melon:* serve chilled in wedges with halved grapes, and have caster sugar and powdered ginger on the table. Melon can also be served with thin raw Parma ham and freshly-milled black pepper

❊ ⬤ Fresh Fruit in Cream and Vinaigrette   *(serves 4)*

2 dessert apples
2 pears
The juice of ½ lemon
2 oranges
¼ lb. of grapes (approx.)
1 level teaspoon of salt
Freshly-ground black pepper

1 tablespoon of fresh chopped mint or 1 teaspoon of dried
4 tablespoons of wine vinegar
6 tablespoons of olive or groundnut oil
4 tablespoons of single cream

Without removing their skins, cut the apples and pears into quarters, then dice them into cubes. Put them into a bowl and pour over the lemon juice – so that they won't discolour. Peel the oranges, cut them into chunks and add them to the apples and pears. Now add the grapes, which should be halved and de-pipped, into the bowl together with some mint sprinkled over. Cover the bowl with foil and chill for 2 to 3 hours. Meanwhile, make the dressing. Start by putting the salt, pepper and vinegar into a bowl and let it stand for a ½ hour so that the salt can dissolve. Then add the oil. Whisk to mix everything and stir in the cream. Serve the fruit in individual glasses or fruit dishes with the sauce poured over.

◇ Avocado Mousse with Prawns   *(serves 6)*

¼ pint of hot chicken stock (Knorr instant)
½ oz. of powdered gelatine
2 ripe avocados
The juice of ½ lemon
1 clove of garlic, chopped finely

¼ pint of double cream, whipped lightly
¼ pint of mayonnaise
Salt and freshly-milled pepper
4 oz. of frozen prawns,
¼ pint of vinaigrette dressing (see p. 134)

Into the liquidiser goblet put the chicken stock and gelatine and blend for a few seconds till the gelatine is dissolved. Now add the roughly chopped pulp of the 2 avocados (make sure you scrape out the darker green part next to the skin, because this enhances the colour of the mousse). Throw in the lemon juice and garlic as well and blend again till it's all smooth and free of lumps. Next empty the contents into a bowl and stir in the whipped cream and mayonnaise very thoroughly. Season with salt and pepper. Pour into a lightly oiled mould and chill (covered) in the fridge till set. Serve in wedges with a few prawns scattered over, and hand round the vinaigrette dressing.

❋ Shrimp Pâté   *(serves 4)*

6 oz. of frozen potted shrimps
1 oz. of softened butter
3 2½ oz. jars of bloater paste
Freshly-grated nutmeg

Freshly-ground black pepper
1 heaped teaspoon of breadcrumbs
Slices of toast or croûtons

Heat the shrimps a little in a saucepan to melt the butter. In a bowl thoroughly blend the softened butter with the bloater paste and then add in the shrimps, a few gratings of whole nutmeg and some black pepper. Pack it all into a dish and press the breadcrumbs over the surface. Chill it for 2 or 3 hours and serve with croûtons or hot buttered toast.

✻✻ 'Homemade' Pâté   (serves 2–3)

2 rashers of bacon
A little dripping, or cooking oil
1 8 oz. can of Swiss pâté
1 clove of garlic, crushed
¼ teaspoon of dried mixed herbs

Freshly-milled black pepper
1 tablespoon of brandy
1 tomato, sliced
Gherkins
Cocktail onions
Hot buttered toast

Fry the bacon rashers in a little dripping until they are fairly crisp and well-done. Then cut them up as small as possible and mix the pieces into the pâté, adding the garlic, herbs, pepper and brandy. Pack the pâté into a small terrine and chill it well. Serve garnished with slices of tomato, gherkins and small silver onions, and eat with hot buttered toast.

✻✻ Kipper Pâté   (serves 4–5)

4 oz. of butter
1 10 oz. packet of frozen kipper fillets
½ a smallish onion
1 tablespoon of fresh parsley
Juice of ½ lemon

A little grated nutmeg
Salt and freshly-milled pepper
Some breadcrumbs
½ lemon, sliced
A few sprigs of watercress
Hot buttered toast

To start, take the butter out of the fridge and let it soften a bit. Cook the kipper fillets according to the instructions on the packet. Drain them and leave them to cool. Finely chop the onions and the parsley. Remove the skins from the kippers (and save them for some deserving cat). Empty the fillets into a large bowl and mash them like mad with a fork until they form a paste. Add the butter bit by bit, continuing to mash. When all is evenly blended, throw in the onion and parsley, lemon juice and a good grating of nutmeg. Season with salt and pepper (be careful with the salt – you'll have to do a bit of tasting here). Select the dish you want to use and press the mixture into it evenly. Sprinkle the top with a few breadcrumbs and decorate it with the other half of the lemon cut into thin slices. Leave it in the fridge or a cool place for 3 or 4 hours. Serve with hot buttered toast and watercress.

✱ Prawn Pâté   (serves 4)

½ lb. of peeled prawns, defrost if frozen
4 teaspoons of olive oil
The juice of 1 small lemon

A few gratings of nutmeg
Salt and a pinch of cayenne pepper
Hot buttered toast

Put the prawns, the olive oil, lemon juice and nutmeg into the liquidiser and blend for a couple of minutes, till you have a smooth paste. Add some salt and a pinch of cayenne pepper according to taste. Empty the pâté into a small basin or terrine, cover with foil, and chill in the refrigerator for 2 or 3 hours. Serve with some hot buttered toast.

✱ Salmon Mousse with Cucumber Soured Cream   (serves 4)

¼ pint of hot water
½ oz. of powdered gelatine
1 tablespoon of lemon juice (instant if you like)
1 7 oz. can of salmon
2 tablespoons of lightly whipped cream

2 tablespoons of mayonnaise
Salt and freshly-milled black pepper
¼ small cucumber
1 5 fl. oz. carton of soured cream
1 whole lemon

Into your liquidiser goblet pour the water, gelatine and the lemon juice. Blend on a low speed for a few seconds to dissolve the gelatine, then add the contents of your can of salmon, broken up a bit. Pour in the oil that goes with it, too. Then blend on a low speed again till all is smooth and creamy. Now empty everything into a large mixing bowl and thoroughly stir in the cream and mayonnaise. Season with salt and pepper and pour the lot into an oiled mould. Cover and chill in the fridge till it's set. To make the sauce, peel the cucumber. Slice it thinly, then chop the slices and add it to the soured cream with some more salt and pepper. Serve the mousse cut into wedges, give everyone a quarter of lemon to squeeze over and hand round the sauce separately.

✳✳ Tuna Fish with White Beans (serves 4)

- 1 14 oz. can of white kidney beans, drained
- 1 large Spanish onion, sliced finely
- ¼ pint of garlic-flavoured Vinaigrette (see p. 134)
- 4 crisp lettuce leaves
- 1 tomato, sliced thinly
- 1 7 oz. can of tuna fish, drained
- Salt and milled black pepper

Mix the beans and onion together. Pour over the garlic dressing and mix very throughly. This can be done well in advance. On to 4 medium-sized plates put first a crisp lettuce leaf and a couple of tomato slices, then a chunk of tuna fish and finally the beaned-onion mixture. Sprinkle with salt and pepper.

✳ Spiced Grapefruit (serves 4)

- 2 large grapefruit
- 2 tablespoons of soft brown sugar
- Some butter
- 2 level teaspoons of ground cinnamon
- 4 black grapes

Halve the grapefruit and with a small sharp knife cut all round each half, easing the flesh away from the skin. Divide it into segments and sprinkle them with the sugar and cinnamon and put a few dabs of butter here and there. Grill them under a medium heat until the sugar is melted and the grapefruit is heated through. Then pop a black grape on to the centre of each one and serve warm.

❋ Escargot

(serves 4)

½ lb. of Normandy butter,
  room temperature
3 cloves of garlic, crushed
The juice of 1 lemon
Salt and freshly-milled black
  pepper
1 small loaf of French bread

2 tablespoons of freshly-
  chopped parsley
*2 dozen snail shells
*2 dozen canned snails,
  drained

*Delicatessens sell packs of the
two together

Pre-heat oven to 450°F (mark 8)

Mix the butter, garlic and lemon juice and season well with
salt and pepper. Mix in the parsley. Then into each snail
shell put first a blob of the butter mixture, then a snail, then
more butter. You can do all this well in advance, provided
you keep the snails in a cool place. When you're ready to
serve take 4 heatproof dishes and put 6 snails on each. Place
them high up in the oven and when they're sizzling after
10–15 minutes, they're ready. This dish should be served
with lots of crusty bread for dunking into the garlic butter.

❋ Prawns with Aïoli

(serves 4)

2 cloves of garlic, crushed
4 tablespoons of mayonnaise
8 oz. of frozen prawns,
  thawed
Paprika

4 oz. of cold cooked rice
  (with 1 teaspoon of ground
  turmeric added to the cooking water)

Mix the garlic with the mayonnaise, then stir in the prawns.
Serve on 4 small dishes, putting first the rice then the prawn
mixture on top. Decorate with a little paprika.

❋ Tomatoes stuffed with Shrimps

(serves 4)

8 medium tomatoes
6 oz. of frozen potted shrimps,
  thawed
2 tablespoons of mayonnaise
1 tablespoon of tomato ketchup
2 or 3 drops of Worcestershire
  sauce

½ a small onion, chopped
  finely
1 heaped teaspoon of parsley,
  finely chopped
Salt and freshly-milled black
  pepper
Slices of brown bread, butter

With a sharp knife top and tail the tomatoes; scoop out all the seeds and discard them. Place the tomatoes upright on a plate. Mix the shrimps with mayonnaise, ketchup, Worcestershire sauce, onion, parsley and season with salt and pepper. Now stuff the tomatoes with the mixture. It doesn't matter if the stuffing comes over the edge – in fact it looks rather nice. Serve with thinly sliced buttered brown bread.

❊ Crab Cocktail   (serves 6)

2 heaped tablespoons of mayonnaise

3 tablespoons of tomato ketch-up

2 dashes of lemon juice, instant

2 dashes of Worcestershire, sauce

3 dashes of dry sherry

½ cucumber, diced

1 small packet of frozen King crab meat, thawed

1 small packet of dressed crab, thawed

Paprika

4 lemon slices

Slices of brown bread, buttered

Mix the mayonnaise, ketchup, lemon juice, Worcestershire and sherry into a sauce. Then into cocktail glasses put first the diced cucumber, the the King crab, the dressed crab and finally the sauce. A sprinkle of paprika and a slice of lemon on the edge of the glass will make it look as if you've really tried. Serve with some thinly-sliced buttered brown bread.

❊ Tomato salad   (serves 4)

8 large firm tomatoes, thinly sliced

4 heaped teaspoons of onion, finely chopped

4 level tablespoons of parsley, finely chopped

1 heaped teaspoon of dried basil

Vinaigrette dressing (see page 134)

Some crusty French bread

Don't prepare this salad too far in advance – slice the tomatoes about an hour before you need them if you like, and put the dressing on at the last minute. Medium-sized plates (the flat kind) are best for these. Arrange the slices of tomato with the onion, parsley and basil sprinkled over, pour on the dressing and serve with fresh crispy bread.

✳ Salad Niçoise

(serves 4)

3 inches of cucumber, sliced
4 tomatoes, sliced
1 10 oz. can of new potatoes, drained and sliced
2 tablespoons of onion, finely chopped
2 hard boiled eggs, quartered
1 2½ oz. can of anchovies
1 7 oz. can of tuna fish, well drained
1 oz. of small, firm black olives
2 tablespoons of parsley, finely chopped
½ pint of Vinaigrette dressing with garlic (see page 134)

Individual salad or soup bowls are best for this, but medium-sized plates will do. Start by arranging the slices of cucumber and tomatoes at the bottom of the salad bowls. Next put in the sliced potato and a little of the chopped onion. Divide the tuna fish into four and add one quarter on to the centre of each salad. Put two quarters of egg on either side of the tuna, then arrange the anchovies in a square or criss-cross pattern. Next dot a few black olives here and there, sprinkle on the rest of the chopped onion and, finally, the chopped parsley. Prepare a few hours before serving, if you like, but don't put the dressing on till the last moment.

✳ Hors d'oeuvres

(serves 4)

4 crisp lettuce leaves
1 small jar of pickled beetroot, chopped
1 7½ oz. can of Potato salad (Heinz)
1 7½ oz. can of Vegetable salad (Heinz)
1 2½ oz. can of sardines
1 3 oz. can of tuna fish
8 slices of Italian salami
8 black or green olives
2 tomatoes, cut into quarters
½ pint of Vinaigrette dressing (see p. 134)

On a large plate, attractively arrange the lettuce, beetroot, potato salad, vegetable salad, sardines, tuna, salami, olives and tomato quarters and let everyone serve themselves. Serve the dressing separately.

❋ Selection of Cold Meats   *(serves 4)*

8 slices of salami (Italian preferably)
8 slices of Mortadella
8 slices of garlic sausage
8 slices of ham, Prosciutto, if you can get it

2 tomatoes, cut into quarters
8 olives, green of black
Some plain mixed pickles
1 small loaf of bread
Some butter

Arrange the sausage meats, ham, tomatoes, olives and pickles on 4 medium-sized plates and serve with hot fresh bread and creamy butter.

❋❋ Chef's Salad   *(serves 4)*

8 oz. of diced cooked chicken
1 small onion, chopped small
4 sticks of celery, chopped small
1 large, or 2 small dessert apples

The juice of 1 lemon
4 tablespoons of mayonnaise
Salt and freshly-milled black pepper
A little freshly chopped parsley

Into a large mixing bowl put first the diced chicken, then the onion and the celery. Core, quarter and dice the apple(s) but don't remove their skins. Toss the fruit in the lemon juice to prevent it discolouring. Now mix in the apple with the other ingredients, stir in the mayonnaise and add salt, pepper and serve in small dishes sprinkled over with fresh chopped parsley.

❋ Prawns with Celery and Apple   *(serves 4)*

8 oz. of frozen prawns, thawed
4 sticks of celery, chopped small
4 tablespoons of mayonnaise

2 large dessert apples, chopped but not peeled
Salt and freshly-milled black pepper
4 sprigs of watercress

Mix the prawns, celery, apples, salt and pepper evenly together with the mayonnaise. Pile the mixture into tall glasses and serve with a sprig of watercress on top.

✻ Herring and Apple Salad (serves 4)

4 slices of Pumpernickel bread
(or thin brown bread if
you can't get that)
4 pickled herrings (Sainsburys
are good)
4 thin slices of Spanish onion

4 whole slices of dessert apple,
cored
1 5 fl. oz. carton of soured
cream
A pinch of paprika
A little chopped parsley

Place a slice of bread on each of 4 small plates. Then on top
of each put a herring, folded into three, some onion, a slice
of apple and lastly a dollop of soured cream. Add a pinch
of paprika and some chopped parsley to make it look irresistible.

✻ Avocado Vinaigrette (serves 4)

2 ripe avocados
2 crisp lettuce leaves
1 teaspoon of parsley, chopped

¼ pint Vinaigrette dressing,
(see p. 134)

Take the avocados and slice them in half lengthwise, removing the stones. Lay each half on a crisp lettuce and pour the
Vinaigrette dressing into the centre of each cavity. Garnish
with a sprinkling of parsley. If you have any Vinaigrette left
over, pour it into a jug and set it on the table in case more
is needed.

✻ Egg Mayonnaise (serves 4)

4 eggs
2 pickled cucumbers
1 oz. firm black olives
4 tablespoons of mayonnaise
(Hellmans' is good)

4 pinches of paprika
1 teaspoon of parsley, fresh
chopped
(or ½ teaspoon dried)

Hard boil the eggs by placing them in a saucepan of *cold*
water, bring to the boil and allow to simmer for 7 minutes.
Then place them under a tap of running cold water until they
are cold. This way you'll get no dark rims round the yolks.
Peel and halve the eggs, arrange them on small plates with

slices of pickled cucumber. Spoon over each arrangement a tablespoonful of mayonnaise, and sprinkle on the paprika and a little parsley. Finish off with a few black olives here and there.

List of Recipes

FISH

Whether man, woman or beast (with the possible exception of cats) we could all do with a little more fish in our diets. I think we often tend to neglect fish because of its bland nursery-food associations, which is a pity because it's crammed full of valuable nutrients, it's cheaper than meat and is so versatile, lending itself to so many easy to cook dishes.

Unless you live fairly near the coast it's extremely unlikely that you'll ever get 'landed the same day' fish but if you have a reliable fishmonger in your area, it should be fresh enough. There are all sorts of visible clues to the freshness of fish – bright eyes, firm flesh, tight scales – but perhaps the most obvious clue (since few of us get the chance to study matters in that detail when it's our turn in the queue) is whether or not your fishmonger is sold out by the early afternoon. A jam-packed slab at four o'clock is a bad omen. Obviously, fresh fish or shellfish won't always be as convenient to use as frozen (you can't ask the fishmonger to peel your prawns, yet don't hesitate to ask him to clean,

✳ Cook-ahead ✱ Up to 30 mins ◆ Over 30 mins

bone, scale and skin), but you'll have a far greater range at your disposal and will find a few recipes in this chapter which can only be made with fresh fish.

The good thing about frozen fish, whatever the weather or season, good landings or bad, is that it's always there, and the prices are always stable. Most frozen fish can be cooked while it's still frozen hard and there's no tiresome boning and cleaning involved. In recent years whole new vistas of frozen fish have been opened up to the inland housewife from salmon fish fingers to rainbow trout. Prawns seem to come in no less than three sizes: normal, huge and king-sized; crab comes dressed or plain and scallops, now packed in bags without their shells, are effortless to cook. If you have to give a quick gourmet meal at short notice, there's no doubt that frozen fish is your best bet. Take careful note of timings on the back of packets. You'll find that the following recipes don't include ready-crumbed fish. The trouble is that most brands insist on covering them with bright orange crumbs, and that's a dead give-away. Most delicatessens and fishmongers sell uncoloured breadcrumbs, and it's so easy to coat the fish yourself – and a lot more realistic.

No well-stocked store-cupboard is complete without a stash of canned fish. Canned sardines come in handy when served along with a little basil sprinkled on tomato slices as a starter, so do large tomatoes stuffed with tuna fish. Tuna can also be transformed into a pâté with some butter and a little chopped onion, and, flaked, it is an automatic choice for a summer lunch salad. While you're hunting round delicatessens, watch out for canned herring or mackerel fillets in various sauces. Prawns, shrimps, crab and lobster all come in cans, and you can get mussels and cockles in glass jars – it's so easy to make a quick seafood risotto with a couple of cans of shellfish and a can of Spanish rice. Pickled herrings are cheap (both Sainsburys and Marks and Spencer are particularly good); always keep them in the refrigerator, though, along with smoked cod's roe and other fish spreads. You'll find details of treating and serving smoked fish of all sorts in the chapter on Starters.

❈ Baked Fish Fingers ⸱(serves 4)

1 14 oz. packet of frozen fish fingers

Salt and freshly-milled black pepper

1 tablespoon of lemon juice

1 6½ oz. can of tomatoes, drained

1 medium-sized onion, sliced thinly

1 7½ oz. can of grilling mushrooms, drained

2 oz. of Cheddar cheese, grated

A little butter

Pre-heat oven to 350°F (mark 4)

Butter a fireproof baking-dish and arrange the fish fingers in it. Season with salt and pepper and sprinkle on the lemon juice. Now cover the fish fingers with tomatoes, onions, and mushrooms. Sprinkle with the grated cheese and put a few dabs of butter here and there. Bake for 20–25 minutes.

❈ Cod Baked in Foil (serves 4)

1 lb. of deep frozen cod fillets, thawed, or 1lb. of fresh cod

Salt and freshly-milled black pepper

Some butter and cooking oil

2 tablespoons of lemon juice

1 3½ oz. can of crab

½ 10 oz. can of Cream of Mushroom soup

A little nutmeg

1 tablespoon of dry sherry

Pre-heat oven to 350°F (mark 4)

Cut the fish fillets into 4 pieces and dry them with some kitchen paper. Sprinkle with salt and pepper and fry in a mixture of oil and butter until they're golden brown. Transfer them on to a largish sheet of buttered foil and sprinkle with lemon juice. Now take a small saucepan and heat the crab meat in a little melted butter, add some nutmeg and sherry. Spread the crab mixture over the cod fillets, pour over the soup and wrap up the foil carefully so that no juices can escape. Bake for 15 minutes.

✻ Cod Portugaise (serves 4)

1½ lb. of frozen cod steaks, thawed

1 tablespoon of flour, seasoned with salt and pepper

Olive oil

2 medium-sized onions, chopped

2–3 cloves of garlic, crushed

1 5 oz. can of sweet red peppers, drained and chopped

1 6½ oz. can of tomatoes

Salt and freshly-milled black pepper

1 tablespoon of fresh chopped parsley

Pre-heat oven to 400°F (mark 6)

Cut each cod steak into 4 pieces and toss them in the seasoned flour. Fry them quickly in hot oil to brown them lightly. Then using a draining-spoon transfer them into a casserole. Now fry the onions and garlic till a pale gold, add the chopped peppers and tomatoes and season with salt and freshly-milled black pepper. Pour it all over the fish and bake in the oven for about 10 minutes without covering. Serve with chopped parsley sprinkled over.

✻ Cod Steaks in Cider (serves 4)

1½ lb. of frozen cod steaks, thawed

1 tablespoon of flour, seasoned with salt and pepper

Salt and freshly-milled black pepper

¼ pint of dry cider

1 medium-sized onion, chopped small

1 clove of garlic, crushed

1 oz. of butter

1 6½ oz. can of tomatoes

Fresh parsley, chopped

Dry the cod steaks and give them a light coating of seasoned flour. Put them into a shallow saucepan and pour in the cider. Fry the onion and garlic in the butter till soft, and add the tomatoes. Let it all come to simmering point, then pour into the saucepan with the fish. Cover with a lid and heat to boiling point. Simmer for 10 minutes, then remove the lid and simmer for a further 10 minutes. Sprinkle with fresh chopped parsley before serving.

✳ Fish Steaks with Cheese and Celery (serves 4)

1½ lb. of frozen cod steaks, thawed
Freshly-milled black pepper
½ 5 oz. can of Condensed Celery soup
2 tablespoons of milk
1 tablespoon of lemon juice

3 tablespoons of Cheddar cheese, grated
2 tablespoons of spring onions, chopped
A little paprika
1 oz. of butter

Pre-heat oven to 425°F (mark 7)

Butter a baking dish and arrange the cod steaks in it; season them with a little freshly-milled black pepper. Mix the soup and milk thoroughly and evenly (the rest of the soup you'll have to keep for another day). Add the grated cheese, spring onions and lemon juice to the soup mixture then pour it all over the fish. Sprinkle with paprika and dot with a few flecks of butter. Bake for 20–25 minutes.

✳ Florentine Plaice Fillets (serves 4)

1 8 oz. large packet of frozen chopped spinach, thawed and drained
Salt and freshly-milled black pepper
1 13 oz. packet of frozen plaice fillets, thawed
¼ whole nutmeg, grated

½ pint of instant cheese sauce
2 oz. of grated Cheddar cheese
1 heaped teaspoon of grated Parmesan cheese
1 tablespoon of packet breadcrumbs
Some butter

Pre-heat oven to 350°F (mark 4)

Butter a shallow baking-dish and arrange the spinach in it. Season with salt and freshly-milled black pepper. Now arrange the frozen plaice fillets on top and season again with more salt and pepper. Add the nutmeg to the cheese sauce (made according to the instructions on the packet). Pour it over the plaice and spinach and sprinkle with grated Cheddar cheese, Parmesan and breadcrumbs. Dot with flecks of butter and bake high in the oven for about 20 minutes.

Plaice Fillets with Prawns and Mushrooms (serves 4)

4 plaice fillets, thawed if frozen or fresh

3 oz. of butter

½ oz. of flour

Salt and freshly-milled black pepper

¼ pint of milk

1 tablespoon of single cream

1 7½ oz. can of grilling mushrooms, drained

2 oz. of prawns (thawed if frozen) or fresh

A little grated nutmeg

6 level tablespoons of fresh white breadcrumbs (made in a liquidiser)

Pre-heat oven to 350°F (mark 4)

Wipe the plaice fillets and lay them flat, with the flesh sides up, on a well buttered shallow roasting tin or baking sheet. Now take a small thick saucepan and melt ½ oz. of the butter in it, add the flour, salt and pepper and stir with a wooden spoon to blend smoothly. Add a little of the milk blending that in carefully, and go on adding a little at a time till it's all even. Turn the heat to low, letting the sauce bubble for a couple of minutes. Melt a little butter in a frying pan and toss the mushrooms in to cook them slightly. Then add them to the sauce with the prawns. Lastly, add the cream and a little grated nutmeg. Now spoon some of the mixture over each fillet. Melt the rest of the butter and, using a pastry-brush, brush half of it over the fish. Covering the whole lot with fresh breadcrumbs, pour the rest of the butter over the crumbed contents and bake for 25 minutes.

❀ Provençale Plaice Fillets (serves 4)

4 tablespoons of packet breadcrumbs, uncoloured if possible

2 cloves of garlic, finely chopped

¼ teaspoon of thyme

3 tablespoons of finely chopped parsley

Grated peel of a ½ lemon

1 egg, beaten

Salt and freshly-milled black pepper

4 oz. of butter

8 small frozen plaice fillets, thawed

1 level teaspoon of paprika

Pre-heat oven to 450°F (mark 8)

Mix together the breadcrumbs, garlic, thyme, parsley and

lemon peel. Beat up the egg and season it well with salt and freshly-milled black pepper. Now grease a baking tin with plenty of butter, reserving 2 oz. for melting in a small saucepan over a low heat. Dip each plaice fillet first into beaten egg, then into the breadcrumbs mixture (making sure each one gets a good coating). Lay the fillets flat on the baking tin, sprinkle the paprika on them and pour over the butter. Let them bake for 12 minutes. Serve with sautée potatoes, a crisp green salad and lemon quarters to squeeze over.

❋ Devilled Crab (serves 4)

1 packet of onion sauce mix
1 oz. of butter
1 teaspoon of dried English mustard
1 tablespoon of Dijon mustard
2 tablespoons of Worcestershire sauce
¼ teaspoon of cayenne pepper
1 lb. King crab meat, frozen

1 5 oz. can of red peppers, drained and chopped
2 hard boiled eggs, chopped
1 tablespoon of parsley, freshly chopped
Salt and freshly-milled black pepper
3 tablespoons of Parmesan cheese, grated

Pre-heat oven to 450°F (mark 8)

Make up the onion sauce according to the instructions on the packet, adding 1 oz. of butter to it. Mix the mustards, Worcestershire sauce and cayenne pepper into it. In a buttered shallow baking tin (or casserole) arrange the crab meat (thawed) cut into chunks, the red peppers and the chopped hard boiled egg. Sprinkle with chopped parsley and season with salt and black pepper. Now pour over the sauce, sprinkle the Parmesan cheese on top and bake in a high place in the oven for 20 minutes.

❋ Fresh Haddock with Cream and Parsley Sauce (serves 4)

1½ lb. of fresh filleted haddock, in 4 portions
Salt and milled black pepper

1 lemon
Parsley sauce (see page 128)

Pre-heat oven to 350°F (mark 4)

Put the haddock portions close together on to a double sheet of foil. Season them with salt and pepper and place 1 thin slice of lemon on each one. Pour over the cream and wrap the foil round securely. Then bake on a heatproof dish for about 30 minutes. Serve with Parsley sauce.

✷ Smoked Haddock with Egg and Cream Sauce (serves 4)

1½ lb. of filleted smoked haddock	2 oz. of butter
Salt and freshly-milled black pepper	½ packet of white sauce mix
	2 tablespoons of double cream
½ pint of milk	1 hard boiled egg
1 bay leaf	1 level tablespoon of chives, fresh chopped (or dried)

Pre-heat oven to 350°F (mark 4)

Divide the haddock into 4 portions, season with salt and pepper and lay them in a baking tin. Pour the milk over and throw in a bay leaf. Put a few flecks of butter here and there. Bake it in the oven for 20–25 minutes. The fish will begin to look slightly opalescent when it's done. Take a fish slice and carefully transfer the fish to a serving dish and put it at the bottom of the oven turned to its lowest (to keep warm). Make up the white sauce mix according to the directions on the packet and, using the milky liquid the fish was cooked in (discard the bayleaf), add the cream, chopped hard boiled egg and chives. Taste to check seasoning and serve the fish with the sauce poured over.

✷ Herrings in Oatmeal with Mustard Sauce (serves 4)

1 or 2 herring per person	Cooking oil and butter
Salt and milled black pepper	1 lemon
4 or 5 tablespoons of medium oatmeal	A few sprigs of fresh parsley
	Mustard sauce (See p. 127)

Pre-heat oven to 350°F (mark 4)

Don't forget to get *medium* oatmeal for this; ordinary porridge oats are too coarse. Ask your fishmonger to bone the herrings and remove the heads and tails. Wipe the fish with a damp cloth, season them with salt and pepper and dip them in the oatmeal, pressing it well in on both sides. Heat a little cooking oil with a knob of butter and fry the herrings for about 4 minutes on each side – they should be nicely browned and crisp. Drain them on crumpled grease-proof paper. Arrange on a platter garnished with lemon quarters and sprigs of parsley and serve with mustard sauce.

✱ Mackerel Stuffed with Green Gooseberries   (serves 4)

4 fresh mackerel
1 tablespoon of flour, seasoned with salt and pepper
A little butter and cooking oil
1 15 oz. can of gooseberries, drained
2 oz. butter

1 heaped tablespoon un-coloured packet bread-crumbs
Salt and freshly-milled black pepper
1 small lemon

Pre-heat oven to 350°F (mark 4)

Ask the fishmonger to clean the mackerel and remove their heads and tails. Wash them under cold running water and dry them thoroughly in a clean cloth or kitchen paper. Now take a sharp knife and make a slit along the backbone to form a pocket. Next, give each one a light dusting with seasoned flour and fry them in a fairly hot mixture of butter and oil, about 5 minutes on each side. This should make the outside skins nice and crisp. Spread a sheet of foil on the bottom of a roasting-tin and place the mackerel pouch side up. Fill each pouch with gooseberries. Sprinkle over the breadcrumbs, salt and pepper, dot with flecks of butter and bake for 20–25 minutes. Serve garnished with a quarter of lemon per serving.

✳ Mediterranean Fish Pie　　　　　*(serves 4)*

1 lb. of frozen haddock, thawed
Salt and freshly-milled black pepper
¼ pint of dry white wine
4 oz. of frozen prawns, thawed
1 7½ oz. can of grilling mushrooms, chopped
1 packet of onion sauce mix
2 oz. of butter
2 tablespoons of fresh chopped parsley
1 packet of instant mashed potato
2 tablespoons of cream, or top of the milk
3 oz. of Cheddar cheese grated
A little paprika

Pre-heat oven to 400°F (mark 6)

Poach the haddock, seasoned with salt and pepper, in the white wine for 10 minutes. Then drain, reserving the liquid for later. Flake the fish and arrange it in the bottom of a well buttered pie dish, and scatter around the prawns and mushrooms. Now make up the onion sauce according to the instructions on the packet, adding the fish liquor to the amount of liquid required. Add half the butter to the sauce and stir in the chopped parsley. Next pour the sauce evenly over the fish. Make up the mashed potato as directed, adding the cream, the rest of the butter and the grated Cheddar cheese. Spread the mashed potato on top of the fish (and if you like make patterns in the top). Sprinkle paprika over and bake for 20–25 minutes, or until the top is golden. Serve with a plain green salad.

✳ Scampi Provençale　　　　　*(serves 4)*

2 oz. of butter
1 medium-sized onion, chopped small
1 clove of garlic, crushed
½ glass of dry white wine
1 6½ oz. can of tomatoes
1 level teaspoon of concentrated tomato purée
1 lb. of frozen Scampi, thawed
1 7½ oz. can of grilling mushrooms, drained and chopped
1 tablespoon of fresh parsley, chopped
Salt and milled black pepper

Melt the butter and fry the chopped onion and garlic in it to soften. Add the wine, tomatoes and tomato purée and cook for about 15 minutes, until the liquid has reduced slightly. Now add the scampi and mushrooms and cook for another 10 minutes. Season to taste and serve with rice and a garnishing of parsley.

SALMON

Cooking salmon is so easy even a child can do it, and during the summer months, when it's no dearer than good quality steak, it's ideal for a special lunch or dinner. The following recipes will show you several ways of cooking fresh salmon very easily – and I promise you the results will be as good as those of any highly-qualified chef anywhere in the world.

❋ Baked Salmon   (serves 4)

1½ lb. of fresh middle-cut   3 bay leaves
  salmon, either in one piece 2 oz. of butter
  or 4 steaks
Salt and milled black pepper

Pre-heat oven to 250°F (mark ½)

If you use salmon steaks, leave the skins on and put them together to form the original piece. Season with salt and freshly-milled black pepper. Put the bay leaves into the centre cavity with half the butter, and put the other piece of butter on top. Wrap a double sheet of foil carefully round the fish, sealing the salmon inside. Place on a heat-proof plate and bake for 1 hour exactly. (When cooked the skin will come away very easily). This is the standard way of cooking salmon. If you're serving it cold, remove it from the oven and *leave* it in the foil to get quite cold. If you don't unwrap it until you're ready to eat it, it will keep beautifully moist.

❋ Baked Salmon with
Cucumber Sauce   (serves 4)

2 oz. of butter   Salt and freshly-milled black
½ pint of milk   pepper
½ cucumber, peeled and   1½ lb. of salmon, baked
  sliced thinly   (see above)
½ packet of white sauce mix   4 lemon quarters

Melt the butter in a small pan, add the milk and gently stew the cucumber in it for about 10 minutes. Make up the white sauce mix according to the instructions on the packet, then add the cucumber and butter in which it was cooked. Season with salt and pepper and serve the salmon hot (with the juices it was cooked in) and the sauce separately. Garnish with lemon quarters.

✱ Chilled Salmon with Avocado Sauce

(serves 4)

½ medium-sized avocado pear
1 tablespoon of lemon juice
1 small clove of garlic, crushed
Salt and freshly-milled black pepper

1 5 fl. oz. carton of soured cream
1½ lb. of cold baked salmon (See opposite)
Lemon wedges

Scrape all the flesh from the avocado, making sure you get all the very green part next to the skin. Mash it to a smooth pulp with a fork and add the lemon juice, garlic, salt and freshly-milled black pepper. Mix in the soured cream and serve this delicious pale green sauce with the chilled salmon and lemon wedges.

✱ Cold Salmon with Cucumber Soured Cream

(serves 4)

½ medium cucumber, peeled and chopped small
1 5 fl. oz. carton of soured cream
Salt and freshly-milled black pepper

1 heaped teaspoon of mint freshly-chopped
1½ lb. of cold baked salmon (See opposite)
4 crisp lettuce leaves
Lemon quarters

Mix the cucumber and soured cream. Season with salt and pepper and sprinkle with chopped mint. Serve the cold salmon on some crisp lettuce leaves garnished with lemon quarters. Serve the sauce separately.

✳ Sole with Shrimps (serves 4)

8 fillets of sole
Salt and freshly-milled black
  pepper
1 dessertspoon of anchovy
  essence

1 4 oz. packet of frozen
  shrimps or prawns, thawed
½ pint of white sauce, from a
  packet
1 oz. of butter

Pre-heat oven to 375F° (mark 5)

Butter a baking dish and lay the sole fillets out flat on it.
Season with salt and pepper and dot them with flecks of
butter. Cover with buttered foil or greaseproof paper and
bake for 10 minutes. Take off the paper, then add the
anchovy essence and shrimps to the white sauce and pour it
all over the fish. Fleck once again with butter and bake for
another 10 minutes. Serve with plain boiled potatoes.

✳ Sole Veronique with Iced Grapes (serves 4)

8 fillets of Dover sole
Salt and freshly-milled black
  pepper
4 tablespoons of dry white
  wine
1 oz. of butter

½ packet of white sauce mix
1 tablespoon of lemon juice
¼ lb. of white grapes, halved,
  peeled, de-pipped and
  chilled

Pre-heat oven to 400°F (mark 6)

Generously butter a large baking dish. Place the fish fillets
in it folding each one in three. Season with salt and pepper,
then sprinkle over half the wine. Cover with a piece of
buttered foil or greaseproof paper and bake for about 10
minutes. Meanwhile, prepare the sauce according to the instructions on the packet, add to it the rest of the wine,
butter, lemon juice and season with salt and pepper. To
serve, take a fish slice, transfer the fillets on to a warm
serving dish, strain the juices into the sauce and pour it over
the fish. Garnish with ice-cold white grapes.

❋ Baked Trout with Almond Butter (serves 4)

4 frozen trout, thawed
1 tablespoon of flour, seasoned with salt and pepper
2 oz. of melted butter
2 oz. of butter
2 oz. of flaked almonds

Juice of ½ lemon
4 sprigs of watercress
Lemon wedges
Salt and freshly-milled black pepper

Pre-heat oven to 450°F (mark 8)

Dry the trout thoroughly in a clean cloth or some kitchen paper, and dust with seasoned flour. Brush a baking sheet with melted butter, lay the trout on it and pour more melted butter over them. Bake high up in the oven for about 10 minutes, until they're golden brown. Meanwhile, heat up the rest of the butter in a small pan and fry the almonds in it till they're a pale golden brown, add the lemon juice and season with salt and pepper. Serve the fish with the almond butter poured over, garnished with watercress and wedges of lemon.

❋ Poached Trout with Herbs (serves 4)

4 trout, frozen or fresh
Salt and whole peppercorns
4 bay leaves
1 small onion, peeled and cut in rings
1 lemon

1 level dessertspoon of thyme
2 tablespoons of parsley, finely-chopped
1 glass of dry white wine
2 oz. of butter

Get hold of a large frying-pan (or roasting tin) and lay the trout in it. (Don't worry if they're frozen solid, it simply means a bit extra cooking time.) Now sprinkle over them a little salt and throw in the peppercorns. Add the bay leaves, one in between each trout. Lay the onion rings over the top, cut half the lemon into slices and arrange them here and there. Sprinkle the thyme and 1 tablespoon of the chopped parsley over everything. Finally, add the wine and enough cold water to just cover the fish. Bring it to the boil on top of the stove and let it simmer gently for 20 minutes if the trout were frozen or 6 minutes if they were fresh. In a small basin, mix the remaining tablespoon of parsley with the butter and divide into 4 portions. When the trout are ready, carefully lift them out with a fish slice, allowing each one to drain for a few seconds. Serve garnished with parsley butter and wedges of lemon.

❀ Supermarket Paella (serves 4)

1 large Spanish onion, chopped small
1 clove of garlic, crushed
2 tablespoons of olive oil
¼ packet of frozen peas, cooked and drained
1 5 oz. can of red peppers, drained and chopped.

1 15½ oz. can of Spanish rice
8 oz. of fresh peeled prawns, thawed
Meat from 2 cooked chickens portions, chopped
1 7½ oz. can of grilling mushrooms, drained and chopped
Salt and freshly-milled pepper

In a large frying-pan, fry the onion and garlic in the oil for about 15 minutes. Then stir in the rice, peas, peppers, prawns, chicken meat and mushrooms and heat through, stirring most of the time. Taste to check the seasoning before serving.

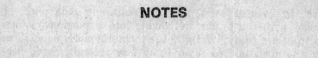

NOTES

List of Recipes

CHICKEN AND DUCK

Now that we can buy ready-cooked chickens practically anywhere, it's possible to cheat like mad with most chicken dishes. Mind you, any old cooked chicken won't do – if it has been hanging around too long (and you'd be surprised how long some of them have) it will probably be too dry. So try and find a reliable cooked chicken dealer and make friends with him, so he can let you know when he's likely to have freshly cooked ones. If the skins get too brown and shrivelled, remove them; they come off quite easily. This chapter deals largely with some of the hundreds of things you can do with ready-cooked chicken, but I've no doubt you will soon be inventing lots of ways of your own. It also contains some suggestions for duck, which of course is easier to obtain frozen than fresh. All the same, it's much more advisable to get one fresh if you can: frozen ones do tend to be a bit on the soggy side when they're thawed, and don't finish up as nice and crisp as fresh ones. Most butchers will get you a fresh duck if you order it well in advance, and it's perfect to serve at a dinner party, since it never spoils if your guests are late or you leave it too long. But remember, one duck only serves four people, so if you're having six to dinner you'll have to buy two and eat half of one cold the next day.

❋ Cook-ahead   ❋ Up to 30 mins   ❋ Over 30 mins

❈❈ Chicken with Red Wine   (serves 4)

5 rashers of bacon, chopped
2 onions, chopped
1 clove of garlic, crushed
1 7½ oz. can of grilling mushrooms
1 bay leaf
½ teaspoon of mixed herbs
Salt and freshly-milled pepper

½ pint of red wine
1 ready-cooked chicken,
 medium-sized
1 dessertspoonful of cornflour
Some water
1 can of Spanish rice
 (optional)

Fry the bacon, onions and garlic in a saucepan. When the onion is soft, add the mushrooms, bay leaf, herbs and seasoning (watch it, though, there's salt in the bacon). Now pour in the wine, turn the heat down and let it simmer and reduce a bit. Take off all the tell-tale shrivelled chicken skin and joint the chicken with a pair of scissors (dressmaking ones are fine) into 4 or 8 pieces. Take the sauce off the heat and thicken it a little with the cornflour mixed with water. Dunk all the chicken pieces in it, and gently reheat until the chicken is warmed through for about 10 minutes. A can of Spanish rice heated through makes a very acceptable accompaniment.

❈❈ Chicken Casserole   (serves 4)

1 cooked chicken, jointed
1 10 oz. can of carrots,
 drained
1 7½ oz. can of grilling mushrooms, drained
1 ¼ lb. packet of frozen peas
½ teaspoon dried tarragon

1 10 oz. can of Condensed
 Chicken soup
¼ pint water
1 tablespoon of instant onion
 flakes
2 packages frozen broccoli,
 optional

Put the chicken, carrots, mushrooms, peas, soup, water and onion flakes into a saucepan, bring the mixture to simmering point and simmer for 15 minutes. This dish is nice with frozen broccoli (cooked of course).

❀ Chicken Basque Style

(serves 4)

1 cooked chicken, jointed
Salt and freshly-milled black pepper
3 oz. of butter
2 medium onions, chopped
1 green pepper, roughly chopped

Some butter and oil
1 14 oz. can of tomatoes
1 level teaspoon of concentrated tomato purée
½ teaspoon of dried thyme
4 slices of fresh orange
1 clove of garlic, crushed

Pre-heat oven to 350°F (mark 4)

Pop the chicken joints into a roasting tin. Season them with salt and pepper and put a knob of butter on each one. Now shove them in the oven to warm through for about 20–25 minutes. Meanwhile you can make the sauce: gently fry the onions and pepper in a little butter and oil till they're soft for 10–15 minutes, then add the tomatoes, tomato purée, thyme and garlic, salt and pepper. Let it all simmer gently for another 10 minutes. Serve the chicken with the sauce poured over and garnish with slices of orange.

❀ Chicken Chasseur

(serves 4)

1 cooked chicken, jointed
4 oz. of butter
2 large onions, roughly chopped
1 clove of garlic, crushed
¼ pint of red wine

½ lb. of dark grilled mushrooms, sliced
1 heaped tablespoon of plain flour
¼ pint of chicken stock (made with a cube)

Pre-heat oven to 350°F (mark 4)

Put the chicken in the oven to warm through with a little butter. Then make the sauce: melt about 2 oz. of butter in a saucepan and gently fry the onions and garlic without letting them brown for about 10–15 minutes. Add the mushrooms, let them cook a little; then with a wooden spoon stir in the flour (quite vigorously so that it doesn't go lumpy). Now add the chicken stock and wine a little at a time, still stirring. Let it all simmer gently for another 10 minutes, then serve the chicken with the sauce poured over it.

✻ Chicken Provençale   (serves 4)

4 cooked chicken joints
2 oz. of butter
2 medium onions, chopped
2 cloves of garlic, chopped
A little olive oil
1 14 oz. can of tomatoes

¼ teaspoon of dried thyme
¾ teaspoon of dried basil
4 oz. of black olives, stoned
Salt and freshly-milled black pepper

Pre-heat oven to 350°F (mark 4)

Put the chicken joints in a meat tin with a knob of butter on each one, and place in the oven to heat through for 20–30 minutes. Make the sauce by frying the onions and garlic in olive oil till soft, say 10 to 15 minutes. Add the tomatoes, herbs and olives. Season with freshly-milled black pepper, then turn the heat up to allow the sauce to bubble and reduce a bit, stirring now and then. Serve the chicken with the sauce poured over.

✻ Chinese Chicken with Pineapple   (serves 4)

(Don't be put off by the list of ingredients – it only takes half an hour)

Some oil and butter
1 medium onion, sliced thinly
1 clove of garlic, chopped
1 tablespoon of flour, seasoned with salt and pepper
1 lb. of cooked diced chicken
1 13 oz. can of pineapple chunks
1 7½ oz. can of grilling mushrooms, drained and chopped

4 oz. of cooked green beans, canned or frozen
1 level tablespoon of soft brown sugar
1 level tablespoon of cornflour
3 tablespoons of malt vinegar
Salt and freshly-milled black pepper
Onion rice (see p. 122)

Heat some oil and butter in a large frying-pan and gently fry the onion and garlic till soft. Toss the chicken pieces in seasoned flour, then stir them in with the onion. Cook for 10 minutes continuing to stir now and then. Drain the pineapple (reserving the juice) and add it to the chicken along with the mushrooms and beans. Stir again, still keeping the heat very low. Now mix the brown sugar and cornflour into a paste with the vinegar. Add the pineapple juice to it and pour the lot into the pan. Then turn the heat up and bring to the boil, stirring all the time. Season to taste, simmer gently for another 8 minutes and serve with onion rice.

�֍ Chicken à la King   (serves 4)

1 pint of onion sauce mix, made up
1 oz. of butter
12 oz. of diced cooked chicken
1 5 oz. can of red pimiento, drained and chopped
1 7½ oz. can of grilling mushrooms, drained and chopped
Salt and freshly-milled black pepper
1 level teaspoon of paprika
3 tablespoons of single cream

Make up the onion sauce according to the instructions on the packet. Add the butter, the chicken, pimiento and mushrooms – and stir. Season with salt and pepper, and with the heat low, give it a chance to heat through – about 10–15 minutes. Before serving add some paprika and cream. Delicious served with rice.

֍ Chicken Pilaff   (serves 4)

1½ oz. of butter
2 onions, chopped small
1 clove of garlic, chopped
1 green pepper, chopped small (or 1 tablespoon of dried)
Salt and freshly-milled black pepper
2 oz. of ready-blanched almonds
8 oz. of long grain rice (Uncle Bens)
1 lb. of diced cooked chicken
¾ pint of chicken stock (Knorr instant)
1 tablespoon of parsley, freshly chopped
1 8 oz. can of pineapple tidbits, well drained

You'll need a largish saucepan for this with a well-fitting lid. In it melt the butter slowly, being careful not to let it brown. Gently sauté the onion, garlic and green pepper for a few minutes to soften; then add the almonds and let them cook for a minute or two. Now stir in the rice and allow it to absorb all the butter and juices. Next add the chicken pieces. Pour in the stock, add some salt and pepper, give one good

stir and put the lid on. Let it simmer *gently* keeping the
heat low. It should cook for about 20 minutes or until all
the liquid has disappeared. Then add the pineapple and let
that heat through (about 10 minutes). Taste to check the
seasoning, and serve with freshly-chopped parsley sprinkled
over. This needs a nice salad to go with it.

✵✿ Chicken Curry   (serves 4)

2 oz. of butter
2 large onions, chopped
1 cooking apples, peeled and
chopped
1 dessertspoon of chutney

2 7½ oz. cans of curry sauce
(Veeraswamy's)
1 ready-cooked chicken, cut
into 4 joints
Salt and freshly-milled pepper

In a large saucepan melt the butter and fry the onions till
soft. Stir in the chopped apple, chutney and seasoning and
let them cook for 2 or 3 minutes. Then pour in the curry
sauce and bring to simmering point. Now add the chicken
joints, spooning the sauce over them. Put on the lid and
let it warm through over a gentle heat for about 20 minutes.

✵✿ Chicken with Bacon and   (serves 4)
Celery

1 ready-cooked chicken
2 oz. of butter
2 medium onions, chopped
4 large sticks of celery,
chopped
2 tablespoons of single cream

6 lean rashers of bacon,
chopped
Freshly-milled black pepper
1 15 oz. can on Cream of
Chicken soup

Take off all the skin from the chicken and discard it. Then
remove all the meat from the bones, taking as large chunks
as possible. In a saucepan melt the butter and gently fry the
onion, celery and bacon for about 15 minutes. Then add the
chicken and some pepper, but no salt because it's already in
the bacon and the soup. Pour in the soup, stir with a wooden
spoon; replace the lid and let it all gently heat through for
a further 15 minutes. At the end stir in the cream. I suggest you serve this dish on a bed of fluffy rice.

☀ Chicken in White Wine with Mushrooms (serves 4)

1 oz. of butter
1 onion, peeled and chopped
1 lb. of cooked chicken in largish pieces
2 7½ oz. cans of grilling mushrooms, drained

Freshly-ground black pepper
1 10½ oz. can of condensed mushroom soup
3 tablespoons of single cream
¼ pint of dry white wine
Grated nutmeg

Heat the butter in a large saucepan and gently soften the onion in it for about 10 minutes. Add the chicken and mushrooms and some freshly-milled black pepper. Pour in the soup, cream and wine and stir well with a wooden spoon to get everything evenly blended. Add a few gratings of nutmeg. Put the lid on and let it simmer gently for 30 minutes. Plain boiled rice is all this needs to go with it.

❋ Chicken Risotto (serves 4)

A little cooking oil
1 large onion, peeled and chopped
1 green pepper, chopped small
½ lb. mushrooms
1 lb. of cooked diced chicken
Salt and milled black pepper

5 oz. of long grain rice (Uncle Ben's)
¼ pint of chicken stock (made from a cube)
4 medium-sized tomatoes
A little fresh parsley, chopped

Pre-heat oven to 350°F (mark 4)

For this you'll need a large frying pan and a casserole. Heat the oil in the pan and gently fry the chopped onion, pepper and mushroom stalks (reserve the tops for later). Add the chicken and some freshly-ground black pepper, but only a little salt (there's some in the stock). Finally, add the rice and stir it with a wooden spoon for a few minutes to absorb all the juices. Transfer all this into a casserole, then pour over the hot chicken stock. Cover it closely and bake for about 40–45 minutes. Meanwhile sauté the mushroom tops (chopped if they're large) in a little oil and quarter the tomatoes and gently fry those. When the risotto is ready, serve it garnished with mushrooms, sautéed tomato quarters and finely-chopped parsley.

◊ Roast Stuffed Chicken   *(serves 4)*

1 3 lb. roasting chicken
4 rashers of fat streaky bacon
2 oz. of butter
Salt and freshly-milled black pepper
½ packet of sage and onion stuffing
4 oz. of pork sausage meat
Bread sauce (see p. 131)

Pre-heat oven to 375°F (mark 5)

If you can only buy a frozen roasting chicken, be very careful to see that it's thoroughly thawed out before you start preparing it for cooking. First of all, make the stuffing according to the instructions on the back of the packet and mix it with the sausage meat. Carefully stuff the breast, being sure not to pack it too tight because it will expand a bit during the cooking. Pull the neck flap down and secure it with a skewer, then put the rest of the stuffing into the body cavity from the other end. Season the chicken with salt and freshly-ground black pepper and rub it all over with the butter. Lay the bacon strips over the breast, put the chicken into a roasting tin and roast it for 1½ hours, basting it a few times. Remove the bacon for the last 20 minutes of the cooking time. Serve with gravy and bread sauce.

At these temperatures an unstuffed chicken will take approximately 20 minutes to the pound plus another 20 minutes to cook; a stuffed bird will need 25 minutes to the pound plus 25 minutes extra.

◊ Roast Chicken with Chestnut Stuffing   *(serves 4)*

1   4 lb. roasting chicken
1 10 oz. can of natural whole chestnuts, drained
Salt and freshly-milled black pepper
6 rashers of streaky bacon
2 oz. of butter
1 onion, chopped very small
1 large cooking apple, peeled and chopped small
4 oz. of pork sausage meat
1 small egg, beaten

Pre-heat oven to 375°F (mark 5)

Prepare the stuffing by chopping the chestnuts and mashing them a little. Season with salt and pepper (but go lightly on the salt as there's already some in the bacon). Chop up 3 rashers of bacon and fry them in butter with the chopped onion, just to melt. Add the sausage meat and onion and chopped apple to the chestnut and mix everything thoroughly. Bind together with a beaten egg, then stuff the bird at both ends. Secure the neck flap underneath with a skewer. Run the butter liberally all over, put 3 rashers of bacon over the breast and roast it for 25 minutes to the pound plus 25 minutes extra, basting now and then. Remove the bacon for the last 20 minutes of cooking.

⚛ Spiced Chicken   (serves 4)

4 chicken portions	1 oz. of butter
1 level teaspoon of curry powder	1 5 fl. oz. carton of single cream
1 level dessertspoon of ground turmeric	1 5 fl. oz. carton of natural yoghurt
1 level dessertspoon of powdered ginger	2 medium onions, roughly chopped
Salt and milled black pepper	Curry rice (see p. 122)

Pre-heat oven to 350°F (mark 4)

About 2 or 3 hours before you start cooking, mix the curry powder, turmeric and ginger together and rub a little of it into each chicken portion. When you're ready to start, put the chicken in a roasting tin, season it with salt and pepper, put a knob of butter on to each portion and put it into the oven to roast for about 30 minutes. Mix the cream, yoghurt and curry spices together in a small basin and fry the onions gently until they're almost cooked. After the 30 minutes are up, spoon the onions over the chicken pieces then pour the cream mixture over and return to the oven to cook for another 45 minutes, basting the chicken a couple of times. Serve the chicken on a bed of curry rice and spoon the sauce over it all. Give each person a small salad of sliced tomato, cucumber and slivers of raw onion.

✪❊ Roast Duck with Cherries   *(serves 4)*

1 largish duck	Salt and freshly-milled pepper
½ 12 oz. jar of Morello cherry jam	Watercress
¼ pint of red wine	

Pre-heat the oven to 425°F (mark 7)

Order your duck well in advance from the butcher -- and ask him to try and get you a fresh one. If you can only get a frozen one, though, make quite sure it's thoroughly defrosted before you start cooking, otherwise a certain amount of water will escape with the fat and it'll all end up a nasty, soggy mess. Duck is a very fatty bird so it's necessary to *overcook* it. Then all the fat will escape and it should turn out a dark nut-brown colour and very crisp on the outside. Put the duck into a roasting tin, prick the fleshy parts with a skewer (to allow the fat to escape) and rub in some salt. Put it fairly high up in the oven just as it is, then after a ½ hour turn the temperature down to 350°F (mark 4) to cook it for 2 hours, during which time drain the fat once or twice from the bottom of the tin. When the 2 hours are up, turn the oven back to 425°F again for about 20 minutes to give the duck a final crisping-up. To serve: cut it into quarters with a pair of scissors (holding it steady with a carving fork). Pour the sauce over it at the very last minute, and garnish with sprigs of watercress. Serve with buttered peas and baby roast potatoes sprinkled with a little crushed rosemary.

✪❊ Cold Duck with Orange Salad   *(serves 4)*

1 cooked duck quartered (cooked as in previous recipe)	4 crisp lettuce leaves
	Rice salad (see p. 121)
2 large oranges	Watercress

Peel the orange, removing as much pith as you can. Slice 1 orange in thin slices and cut the other orange into bite-sized slices (you'll need a very sharp knife for this). Now take a largish serving dish, and put 4 crisp lettuce leaves in the centre with a duck portion on each and garnish with orange slices and watercress. Next mix the orange pieces into the rice salad and arrange it all around the duck. This is a delicious cold dinner-party dish for a very hot summer's evening – if one's lucky enough to get a hot summer's evening.

NOTES

MEAT, STEWS & CASSEROLES

List of Recipes

LIST OF RECIPES

MEAT, STEWS & CASSEROLES

Meat served straight out of a can never really fools anyone. A can of stewed steak tastes like stewed steak. In high-class grocer's shops one can now buy some of the classic dishes deep frozen. They all sound extremely tempting – Duck à l'Orange, Chicken Basque, Boeuf Bourguignonne – but they're *very* expensive and a bit disappointing for the price, I think. What we actually need, then, are ideas for main dishes using both fresh and instant, which enable us to produce worthwhile results with an absolute minimum of effort. That's what this chapter is all about.

First a word about buying meat. Supermarket meats tend, on the whole, to be less good than those bought from the family butcher and certainly more expensive. Meat, don't forget, is subject to seasonal changes in price and quality, and if you make a friend of your butcher you can always ask his advice on best buys. All the same, supermarket steaks,

❋ Cook-ahead   ❋ Up to 30 mins   ◆ Over 30 mins

chops, sausages, bacon joints, liver and kidneys are perfectly acceptable. Where the meat is deep-frozen, always make sure that it's thoroughly thawed before cooking.

The suggestions offered in this chapter fall broadly into three categories: there are those which don't use convenience foods but are *easy* to make and compare favourably with more complicated dishes. Pork with Honey and Ginger, for instance, is infinitely more 'convenient' and equally as good as, say, Roast Lamb with Mushroom Stuffing and Demiglace sauce (which you won't find a recipe for here). Then there are the everyday quickies such as chops, ham, steaks and veal escalopes, for which I have tried to suggest ways of exploiting the range of products available from most supermarkets. Rather than attempt to turn them into classic dishes, you're really better off looking for ways and means of glamourising them and providing interest and variety. (I would include here the casseroles and what I call One-Pot recipes that can be made in moments, left to cook slowly, and forgotten till you're ready to serve -- in fact most casseroles improve with hanging around a bit, and are even better eaten the next day).

Finally, there are the canned meats which, as I've indicated, cheats ought to approach with caution. But there are honourable exceptions to this: some canned curries, for example, are reasonably good (Marks and Spencer are excellent), but it is always worth adding some fried onions, a bit of diced apple fried and 1 teaspoon of sweet chutney. Heat up the curry with these added and, if you like, a few pinches of powdered ginger and turmeric. Canned curries always look better served on curry-flavoured rice (see page 122). Chiltern, the herb people, do packets of rice ready flavoured. Always serve the curry with some mango chutney on the table and perhaps sliced banana mixed with natural yoghurt.

✿ Cottage Pie   *(serves 4)*

- 1 15 oz. can of savoury minced beef
- 1 tablespoon of dried minced onions
- 1 small green pepper, chopped
- ½ teaspoon of dried mixed herbs
- Salt and milled black pepper

- 1 15 oz. can of Italian tomatoes, drained
- 1 packet of instant mashed potato
- 2 oz. of grated Cheddar cheese
- Some butter

Pre-heat oven to 350°F (mark 4)

Grease a pie-dish with a butter paper. Mix together the mince, onions, chopped green pepper and mixed herbs. Season with freshly-milled black pepper. Pack the lot into the bottom of the pie-dish and arrange the tomatoes on top. Make up the mashed potato according to the instructions on the packet then beat in the grated Cheddar cheese and a knob of butter, and some pepper and salt to taste. Spread the potato over the meat and tomatoes (and make pretty patterns with a fork if you feel like it). Sprinkle the grated Parmesan over and put a few small dabs of butter here and there. Bake it in the oven for 45 minutes.

✿ Ten-minute Meat Loaf   *(serves 4)*

(Well, only 10 minutes in preparation, then you can forget it for 1¼ hours in the oven).

- 1 lb. of lean minced beef (from a reliable butcher) (fatty mince is no good)
- ½ lb. of pork sausage meat
- 2 large onions, chopped very small
- 1 clove of garlic, crushed

- 1 teaspoon of dried mixed herbs
- Salt and freshly-milled black pepper
- 2 slices of bread, crusts off
- 2 tablespoons of milk
- 1 egg, beaten

Pre-heat oven to 375°F (mark 5)

Get out a large mixing bowl and clear off plenty of working space. Put into the bowl the meat, sausage meat, onions, herbs, garlic and plenty of salt and freshly-milled black pepper. Soak the bread in the milk, give it a good squeeze and throw it in with the rest. Now get to work mixing everything as evenly as possible. You'll probably find it's easier to do this with your hands. Mix in a beaten egg to bind it all together, then pack it into a 2 lb. loaf-tin and bake for 1¼ hours. It's delicious served with canned tomato sauce, and just as good eaten cold as it is hot.

✿❈ Moussaka   (serves 6)

2 15 oz. cans of savoury minced beef

2 tablespoons of dried minced onions

1 teaspoon of ground cinnamon

1 clove of garlic, crushed

2 tablespoons of red or white wine (optional)

2 medium-sized aubergines

1 level tablespoon of concentrated tomato purée

Salt and milled black pepper

1 packet of cheese sauce mix

Some butter

Some cooking oil

A little whole nutmeg, grated

2 eggs

A little Parmesan cheese

Pre-heat oven to 350°F (mark 4)

For this you'll need a good-sized casserole without its lid. Start by giving it a going-over with some butter paper. Take a large mixing-bowl and a fork, then mix together the mince, the onions, cinnamon and garlic. Season with salt and a little freshly-milled black pepper. If you have any left-over wine in the cupboard, mix it with the tomato purée (if not use water instead) and pour this over the meat mixture. Have another good old mix round with the fork. Next the aubergines: slice them into thinnish rounds and fry them in oil – you'll need quite a lot of oil because aubergines absorb it in seconds. Now into your buttered casserole go first the meat mixture and then the aubergines spread out on top. Make up the cheese sauce according to the instructions on the packet, adding a knob of butter, a few good gratings of whole nutmeg and some freshly-milled black pepper. Allow the sauce to cool slightly. Whisk the 2 eggs on their own and then into the sauce. Pour the whole lot over the meat and aubergines. Sprinkle some grated Parmesan over the top and bake it for about 45 minutes.

✿ Italian Beef   (serves 4)

1 15 oz. can of Italian tomatoes
2 lb. of best stewing beef, cut into small cubes
1 clove of garlic, crushed
Salt and freshly-milled black pepper

1 large green pepper, roughly chopped
2 large onions, chopped
½ glass of red cooking wine
1 bay leaf
Onion rice (see p. 122)

Pre-heat oven to 300°F (mark 2)

Put half the canned tomatoes in the bottom of a casserole then the meat with the garlic and some salt and pepper. Next add the chopped pepper and onions; then the rest of the tomatoes with the wine. Let it all cook slowly for 3½ hours. This dish is excellent with onion rice.

✿ Beef Pot Roast   (serves 4)

2 lb. of rolled topside or brisket
1 packet of onion soup mix
1 bay leaf
Salt and freshly-milled black pepper

2 standard-sized glasses of red wine
1 15 oz. can of carrots, drained
1 1 lb. 3 oz. can of new potatoes, drained

Pre-heat the oven to 300°F (mark 2)

Take a heavy casserole with a well-fitting lid and put the beef into it. Empty the contents of the packet soup over the beef, throw in the bay leaf and some salt and pepper, then pour the wine over. Put the lid on, then into the oven with it for 2 hours. When the time is up add the drained carrots and potatoes, replace the lid and let it cook for a further 20 minutes.

☿ Lamb Chops Baked with Butter and Herbs (serves 4)

2 oz. of butter, softened
1 clove of garlic, crushed
Salt and freshly-milled black pepper
½ level teaspoon of rosemary, crushed
½ level teaspoon of dried thyme
1 tablespoon of freshly-chopped parsley
4 chump lamb chops

Pre-heat oven to 350°F (mark 4)

In a small basin mix the butter, garlic and herbs and season well with salt and pepper. Put a dab of this herb butter on to each chop and place them in a roasting tin. Let them bake in the oven for 45 minutes, and if you think of it, baste them with the melted butter once or twice.

☿ Barbecued Lamb Chops (serves 4)

4 chump lamb chops
1 medium-sized onion, chopped small
6 tablespoons of barbecue sauce, bottled
4 small blobs of butter
Salt and freshly-milled black pepper
Pilaff rice (see p. 122)

Pre-heat oven to 350°F (mark 4)

Take a meat tin, put your lamb chops into it and sprinkle them with the chopped onion. Pour over the sauce and add a blob of butter to each chop. Into the oven with them for around 45 minutes and season well. These go very well with pilaf rice.

✤ Mustard Glazed Lamb Chops (serves 4)

4 large chump chops
4 heaped teaspoons of mixed mustard (English or French)
Salt and freshly-milled pepper
4 heaped teaspoons of demerara sugar

Wipe the lamb chops, season them with salt and pepper. Spread both sides with mustard and dip both sides in the brown sugar. Grill on both sides, but don't have the heat too high. They should take 20 to 30 minutes, depending on the thickness of the chops.

✳ Savoury Lamb Cutlets   (serves 4)

1 beaten egg
1 dessertspoon of dry English mustard powder
Salt and freshly-milled black pepper
8 best end lamb cutlets
2 tablespoons of flour seasoned with salt and pepper

4 tablespoons of ready-made breadcrumbs
Some cooking oil
½ pint of gravy (from your favourite mix)
1 hard boiled egg, chopped small
2 dessertspoons of Worcestershire sauce

Beat up the egg with the mustard powder, 1 teaspoon of salt and some freshly-milled black pepper. Then dip each cutlet first into the egg mixture, then into the seasoned flour, then in the breadcrumbs to give them a complete coating. Fry the chops in oil – they'll need about 8 minutes each side. Place them on kitchen paper to drain, then serve them with the hot gravy to which you've added the chopped hard boiled egg and some Worcestershire sauce.

◊ Bacon with Parsley Sauce   (serves 4)

1½ lb. Boil-in-the-bag bacon joint
½ dozen cloves
½ packet onion soup mix
1 packet of Parsley Sauce mix

1 oz. butter
1 tablespoon of freshly-chopped parsley
2 tablespoons of double cream

Pre-heat oven to 300°F (mark 2)

Take the joint out of the bag and cut off the polythene strip that holds it all together. Place it on a double sheet of foil, stick the 6 cloves in here and there and empty the half-packet of onion soup all around it. Wrap it up carefully to seal it safely inside. Put it on to a baking tin (in case it leaks) and leave it in the oven for 2½ hours. Just before it's ready, make-up the parsley sauce according to the directions on the packet, adding to it the butter and the double cream. When the time is up turn the bacon out on to a serving dish, fish out the cloves and discard them. Carve the joint and serve it with a little of the gravy and some Parsley sauce.

✿ Ham Baked in Pastry   (serves 4)

1. lb. can of cooked ham
½ lb. of ready-made puff pastry
Cumberland sauce (see p. 133)

1 tablespoon of dry white wine
1 beaten egg yolk and some water

Pre-heat the oven to 450°F (mark 8)

Flour a pastry board and a rolling-pin, and roll out your pastry into a round large enough to wrap the ham in. Place the ham on one half of the pastry, then wet the edges all round with water. Sprinkle the wine over the ham, fold over the pastry and stick the edges together (so it's rather like a huge Cornish pasty). Press round the edges with a fork to seal them well and brush it all with beaten egg. Place it on a baking sheet and bake for 20 minutes. Then reduce the temperature to 375°F (mark 5) and give it another 20 minutes. Serve with Cumberland sauce.

✳ Hawaiian Ham Steaks   (serves 4)

4 round ham steaks
1 tablespoon of ready-made English mustard

4 well-drained pineapple rings
1 tablespoon of demerara sugar
4 sprigs of watercress

Grill the ham steaks for a few minutes each side. Allow them to cool enough to handle, then spread them with mustard and place a pineapple ring on each. Sprinkle the sugar over and brown under a hot grill. Serve with a sprig of watercress on top.

✳ Late-Supper Ham Steaks   (serves 4)

4 thick slices of bread
4 round ham steaks
1 tablespoon of ready-made
French mustard

Some butter
4 slices of cheese
4 well-drained pineapple rings
Freshly-milled black pepper

Toast the bread on both sides, then stand it up in a toast rack so that it doesn't go soggy. Grill the ham steaks for a few minutes on each side. Butter the slices of toast and spread them with mustard. Place a ham steak on each, then a slice of cheese with some pepper and a pineapple ring on top. Place them under the grill till the cheese is bubbling and the pineapple is turning brown.

◊ Pork Chops Baked with   (serves 4)
Cream and Mushrooms

4 medium pork chops
1 teaspoon of dried thyme
1 oz. butter
Salt and freshly-milled black
pepper

1 7½ oz. can of grilling mushrooms, drained and chopped
The juice of 1 small lemon
2 tablespoons of plain flour
1 5 fl. oz. carton double cream

Pre-heat to 375°F (mark 5)

Fry the chops a little on both sides to brown them, then place them on a double sheet of foil in a roasting-tin (keep them fairly close together). Sprinkle them with the thyme and season with salt and freshly-milled black pepper. Then, in the frying pan in which you browned the chops, melt the butter, toss in the mushrooms, add the strained juice of the lemon and the flour, mixing it all round with a wooden spoon till you have a rather pale looking goo. (It's supposed to look like that.) Spoon some of this mixture on to each pork chop, spreading it out a bit, then pour the double cream all over. Now quickly wrap the whole lot up as a parcel, pinching the foil edges tightly together so that it doesn't spring a leak. Pop the parcel into the oven and cook for 1 hour.

✪ Stuffed Pork Chops with Spiced Apple Sauce

(serves 4)

4 medium pork chops
Salt and freshly-milled black pepper
½ 2 oz. packet of sage and onion stuffing

¼ lb. of pork sausage meat
1 7½ oz. can of apple sauce (Hero)
¼ teaspoon of ground cloves
2 pinches of ground cinnamon

Pre-heat oven to 375°F (mark 5)

Fry the pork chops a little to brown them on both sides. Put a large double sheet of foil into a roasting tin and place the chops on it, keeping them as close together as possible. Season with salt and pepper. In a basin mix the sage and onion stuffing according to the instructions on the packet, then mix in the sausage meat using a large fork. When it all looks evenly blended, divide it into 4 portions and put 1 portion on to each chop, spreading it all over. Now wrap up the foil round them (like a parcel) and seal it well. Put it into the oven and leave it there for about 1 hour. While it's cooking open your can of apple sauce, add the spices to it and start to heat it just before the pork chops are done. Unwrap the foil, being careful not to burn your fingers, pour off any excess fat and serve with the apple sauce.

✪ Pork Chops with Spiced Apricots

(serves 4)

4 large pork chops (fairly lean)
Salt and freshly-milled black pepper
1 small onion, chopped small
1 oz. of lard

1 15 oz. can of apricot halves, drained
1 dessertspoon of demerera sugar
1 teaspoon of ground cinnamon

Pre-heat oven to 375°F (mark 5)

Place the pork chops in a meat tin. Season with salt and freshly-milled black pepper and tuck the chopped onion in between and around the chops. Then put a small piece of lard on each one and bake high in the oven for around 45 minutes. When they're cooked take them out of the oven and transfer them to a grilling pan (having pre-heated the grill). Arrange the well-drained apricot halves on top, sprinkle them with the sugar and cinnamon and brown them quickly under the grill.

✧ Roast Pork with Honey and Ginger (serves 4)

1 roasting joint of pork (loin is good). About 2½ lb. if on the bone – and ask the butcher to score the skin for you.	Salt and milled black pepper 1 tablespoon of powdered ginger 2 tablespoons of clear honey 12 whole cloves

Pre-heat oven to 400°F (mark 6)

If you can, prepare this a few hours in advance (it will take all of two minutes!). Put the pork in a roasting tin, season it with salt and pepper and rub the powdered ginger into it, sprinkling a little into the tin underneath it. Now rub the honey all over – sorry about your sticky hands, but it's worth it. Stick the cloves here and there into the outer skin. Then leave it in a cool place for a few hours to soak up all the flavours. Bake the pork just as it is; don't add any extra fat or anything. After 15 minutes turn the oven down to 375°F (mark 5) and cook it for another 1½ hours. A little wine added to the juices at the end makes a nice gravy. And don't worry if it turns black during the cooking: that's the honey caramelising, and it's all quite delicious.

✧ Veal Marengo (serves 4)

1 oz. of butter 2 onions, roughly chopped 2 lb. of cubed veal, lean 1 small green pepper, chopped 1 level teaspoon of dried mixed herbs 1 clove of garlic, crushed	4 level tablespoons of concentrated tomato purée ½ pint of dry white wine or cider Salt and freshly-milled black pepper

Pre-heat oven to 350°F (mark 4)

Melt the butter in a casserole and gently sauté the onions in it. Add the veal and brown it very slightly. Now add the chopped pepper and let that, too, fry a little. Add the herbs and garlic, then stir in the tomato purée, and finally the wine with one last good stir round. Season to taste. Pop the lid on and put it in the oven for approximately 1 hour.

◊ Blanquette of Veal   (serves 4)

A little butter and oil
4 lean rashers of bacon, chopped
1½ lb. of veal, cubed
2 onions, chopped
½ teaspoon of dried mixed herbs

1 bay leaf
Salt and freshly-milled black pepper
1 15 oz. can of mushroom soup
¾ pint of dry white wine or dry cider

Pre-heat oven to 350°F (mark 4)

Heat some butter and oil in a frying-pan but have the heat low (it mustn't get brown). Fry the bacon and veal gently, without letting it colour, for 5–6 minutes, then transfer them into a casserole. Now just as gently fry the onions to soften them a little and put them around the meat. Sprinkle in the mixed herbs, add a bay leaf and season with salt and pepper. Add the soup and the wine. Give it all a good stir and let it cook, with the lid on, for 1½ to 2 hours.

◊ Liver and Bacon Casserole   (serves 4)

1¼ lb. of calves' liver
1 tablespoon of plain flour, seasoned with salt and pepper
Some dripping
2 large onions, chopped
1 10 oz. can of carrots

4 lean bacon rashers
1 dessertspoon of Worcestershire sauce
Freshly-milled black pepper
1 10 oz. can of condensed vegetable soup
¼ pint of water

Pre-heat oven to 350°F (mark 4)

Cut the liver into smallish pieces, which should then be tossed in the seasoned flour. Fry the pieces in dripping to brown slightly then transfer them into a casserole. Add the onions, the carrots and the bacon slices laid on top. Sprinkle some Worcestershire sauce over, and some freshly-milled black pepper. Finally, mix the soup with the water and pour that in. Cover and bake for 1¼ hours.

✿❋ Kidneys in Jacket Potatoes   *(serves 4)*

4 large hot jacket potatoes	4 lean rashers of bacon
4 lambs' kidneys, skinned	Salt and freshly-milled black
A little made-up French	pepper
mustard	2 oz. of butter

Pre-heat oven to 400°F (mark 6)

Most jacket potatoes need about 1 to 1½ hours in a 400°F (mark 6) oven. Prepare the kidneys by removing the skins, spreading them with a little mustard and wrapping each one in a rasher of bacon. Cut the hot cooked potatoes into halves and make a depression in the centre of 4 of them. Season with salt and milled black pepper, put in a knob of butter, then a kidney wrapped in bacon on top. Put these halves into the oven for about 20 minutes, keeping the other 4 warm. Serve by placing the appropriate halves together to form a sort of sandwich. A green salad goes very well with this.

EASY STEWS

The first stew is ideal for everyday, family eating; the second is perfect for a dinner party. Both can be made well in advance and require no last-minute bothering. The third stew is a bit more advanced but still quite easy to make and is equally good for entertaining.

✿❋ Easy Stew 1   *(serves 4)*

2 lb. of good stewing beef,	¼ pint of water
cubed	1 bay leaf
¼ lb. of carrots, sliced	½ teaspoon of mixed herbs
2 large onions, sliced	Salt and freshly-milled black
1 15 oz. can of Oxtail soup	pepper

Pre-heat oven to 300°F (mark 2)

Take a large, heavy casserole with a well fitting lid, then just put the beef, carrots, onions, diluted oxtail soup, the bay leaf, the mixed herbs and seasoning into it, cover and leave in the oven to cook for 3½ hours. Serve with green vegetables.

❀ Easy Stew 2   (serves 4)

2 lb. of good stewing beef, cubed

2 large onions, sliced

2 large carrots, sliced

1 10½ oz. can of condensed Tomato soup

⅓ pint of red wine

1 clove of garlic, crushed

1 bay leaf

½ teaspoon of mixed herbs

Salt and freshly-milled pepper

1 7½ oz. can of grilling mushrooms

Pilaff Rice (see p. 122)

Pre-heat oven to 300°F (mark 2)

Put the beef, onions, carrots, soup diluted with wine, garlic, bay leaf, mixed herbs salt and pepper into a casserole. Secure the lid and let it cook for 3½ hours. Slip in the mushrooms for the last 20 minutes of the cooking time. This one is good served with Pilaff rice.

❀ Mutton and Barley Stew   (serves 4)

2½ lb. of middle neck of mutton, cut into small pieces

2 level tablespoons of flour, seasoned with pepper and salt

2 large Spanish onions, peeled and sliced

1 lb. of scrubbed carrots, sliced

1 tablespoon of pearl barley

Salt and freshly-milled black pepper

1 15 oz. can of Scotch Broth

⅓ pint of water

1 10 oz. can of new potatoes

Pre-heat oven to 300°F (mark 2)

Roll the pieces of lamb in seasoned flour and place in the bottom of your casserole. Scatter the onions and carrots all around them. Sprinkle in the pearl barley and add some salt and freshly-milled black pepper. Pour in the soup, then the water, and bring to simmering point on the top of the stove (with the lid on). Now transfer it to the oven and let it gently stew for about 1¾ hours. When the time is up, throw in the drained new potatoes and give it all another 15 minutes before serving.

ONE-POT CASSEROLES

Actually there's very little cheating with ingredients in these recipes, but they're very easy because you can make them in one pot. There's no complicated routine with frying pans and separate saucepans – everything can be cooked in one pot, which you'll be grateful for when it comes to the washing-up. The best type of pot to use is the cast-iron enamelled kind that you may use on top of the stove as well as inside it.

✿✿ Beef Goulash   (serves 4)

2 large onions, sliced
Some dripping
1½ lb. of best stewing beef, cut into smallish cubes
1 tablespoon of dried red and green pepper
1 6½ oz. can of Italian tomatoes, drained
1 level tablespoon of paprika
1 clove of garlic, crushed

1 level tablespoon of concentrated tomato purée
½ teaspoon of dried mixed herbs
Salt and freshly-milled black pepper
1 heaped tablespoon of flour
¾ pint of beef stock, made from a cube
2 tablespoons of yoghurt

Pre-heat oven to 300°F (mark 2)

Gently fry the onions in dripping in your casserole, just to colour them slightly. Add the beef cubes dried peppers and stir them around with a wooden spoon to brown them all over (don't have the heat too high). Now stir in the paprika, the crushed garlic and tomato purée. Sprinkle in the herbs and season with salt and freshly-milled black pepper. Next stir in the flour, and don't worry if it all looks ghastly at this stage – it's supposed to. Gradually stir in the stock, bring it all to simmering point, then on with the lid and transfer it to the oven for around two hours. To finish off stir in the tomatoes and let them heat through for 10 minutes.

Before serving spoon the yoghurt over the top. It's best with rice or boiled potatoes.

✽✽ Beef Curry (serves 4)

2 medium onions, chopped
1 large cooking apple, peeled and chopped
Cooking oil
1 15 oz. can of stewed steak
1 level teaspoon of ground turmeric
1 level teaspoon of powdered ginger
2 dessertspoons of curry powder, or more
1 dessertspoon of chutney
1 5 fl. oz. carton plain yoghurt
Salt and freshly-milled pepper

Cook the onions and apple in oil till soft. Then add the stewed steak, spices and chutney; bring to simmering point, stirring with a wooden spoon to prevent it sticking. Add the yoghurt and stir again to heat through. Taste and season with salt and pepper and more curry powder if needed. Serve with rice and mango chutney.

✤✽ Lancashire Hotpot (serves 4)

8 cutlets of best end neck of lamb
2 lambs kidneys, skinned cored and chopped
1 15 oz. can of carrots, drained and sliced
Salt and freshly-milled black pepper
1 oz. of butter
1 1 lb. 3 oz. can of new potatoes, drained and sliced
2 large Spanish onions, peeled and sliced
1 bay leaf
½ pint of hot water
1 tablespoon of Worcestershire sauce

Pre-heat oven to 300°F (mark 2)

Dip the cutlets and chopped kidney in the seasoned flour to give them a light coating, then lay them in the bottom of your casserole, cutlets first, then the pieces of kidney tucked here and there. Next put in the slices of carrot, and season with salt and freshly-milled black pepper; now the slices of potato, which should cover everything else overlapping each other. Add a little more pepper, onion and bay leaf then pour in a ½ pint of hot water mixed with 1 tablespoon of

Worcestershire sauce. Finally put a few dabs of butter here and there. Leave in the oven, with the lid on, for 2 hours. Take the lid off, turn the heat up to mark 7 (425°F) and let the top get golden-brown (about 20 minutes).

◐❈ Sort of Stroganoff   *(serves 4)*

2 lb. of all-lean chuck steak
2 medium onions, peeled and chopped
1 10½ oz. can of condensed mushroom soup

2 oz. plain flour, seasoned with salt and pepper
1 5 fl. oz. carton of plain natural yoghurt
A little dripping or cooking oil

Pre-heat oven to 300°F (mark 2)

First cut the chuck steak into very thin slices, about 1½ inches long. Toss the strips in seasoned flour. Heat the fat in the bottom of the casserole and fry the meat to brown it a little; add the onions and continue frying for a few minutes, stirring with a wooden spoon. Stir in the soup, then the yoghurt. Season with some salt and freshly-milled black pepper, put on the lid and cook in the oven for 1½ hours. Serve with rice.

◐❈ Chilli Con Carne   *(serves 4)*

2 oz. of butter
2 Spanish onions, chopped small
1 15 oz. can of minced steak
1 15 oz. can of red kidney beans, drained
1 15 oz. can of tomatoes

1 level dessertspoon of concentrated tomato purée
2 level teaspoons of powdered chilli, or more if you prefer it hot
Salt and freshly-milled black pepper

Melt the butter and fry the onions in it for 10 minutes. Add the steak, kidney beans, tomatoes, tomato purée, chilli powder and keep stirring to heat through. Serve with a mixed side-salad and some crusty bread.

❋ Veal Escalopes with Cream and Mushrooms

(serves 4)

4 large veal escalopes, beaten out flat
2 oz. of butter
2 7½ oz. cans of grilling mushrooms, drained and chopped

1¼ pint carton of double cream
Salt and freshly-milled black pepper
Some whole nutmeg, grated

Sauté the escalopes in the butter till they're golden brown, then transfer them into a serving dish and keep warm. Fry the mushrooms in the same pan to heat through, then stir in the cream, salt and pepper to heat gently without letting it boil. It will go a lovely coffee colour. Stir in a few good gratings of fresh nutmeg and pour over the veal. Serve with plain boiled rice.

❋ Spaghetti Bolognese

(serves 4)

1 lb. of spaghetti
1 15½ oz. can of Bolognese sauce
1 level tablespoon of condensed tomato purée
1 clove of garlic, crushed
2 oz. of butter

1 heaped teaspoon of dried basil
Salt and freshly-milled black pepper
Plenty of grated Parmesan cheese

Cook the spaghetti in lots of boiling salted water for 11 minutes (or according to the instructions on the packet). In another saucepan heat up the sauce, tomato purée, garlic and basil. When the spaghetti is done, drain it in a collander then return it to the pan and toss in 2 oz. of butter. Season with salt and freshly-milled black pepper. Serve it on to warmed plates – if you have trouble separating it, lift it as high as you can; that should do it. Pour some sauce over each portion and have the Parmesan on the table to pass round.

⬦ Quick Canelloni   *(serves 4)*

1 14 oz. can of minced beef
1 clove of garlic, crushed
1 dessertspoon of tomato
   purée
1 level teaspoon of dried basil
1 6½ oz. can of Sauce
   Bolognese (Buitoni)

12 thin pancakes, made from
    instant pancake mix
1 pint of instant cheese sauce,
    make up
A little grated nutmeg
2 tablespoons of grated Par-
    mesan cheese
A little butter

Pre-heat oven to 375° (mark 5)

Butter a baking-dish well. Then in a basin mix the minced beef, garlic, tomato purée and basil. Stir in the bolognese sauce and blend evenly. Spoon the mixture on to the flattened pancakes and roll them up. Place them side by side in the baking dish and pour the cheese sauce over, spreading it out evenly. Grate the nutmeg over the cheese sauce and finally sprinkle on the Parmesan cheese. Dot with a few flecks of butter here and there and bake for 45 minutes.

NOTES

List of Recipes

VEGETABLES

People are unfair to vegetables. The fact is that if the vegetables are interesting enough, the dullest of meals can seem far more imaginative: ratatouille with ordinary lamb chops or a crisp green salad with fish fingers, for instance. There is, of course, no substitute for fresh vegetables if you are going to use them in this way, but then a great many need so little preparation there's no need to take any camouflage measures — cauliflower, broccoli, scrubbed carrots, new potatoes (which taste so much better, by the way, if you leave the skins on) and jacket potatoes. But whatever they are there's no excuse for over cooking them. At long last I do believe the British are beginning to realise that most vegetables don't need stewing for ages in pints of water: green vegetables particularly (even frozen ones) should be crisp and firm and buttery. The one short-cut you could legitimately take, though, is to look out for them

❋ Cook-ahead   ❀ Up to 30 mins   ◆ Over 30 mins

ready-prepared (they come in packs from Marks and Spencer).

No cheat will be very successful in passing off tinned vegetables as fresh, whatever contortions she goes through in the kitchen. Their texture and colour, if not their taste, will always give them away. (But by all means use them for soups, stews or casseroles, remembering that as a rule tinned vegetables are already cooked.) There are exceptions, however, which you'll find quite acceptable served on their own with a minimum of disguise: chopped spinach is reasonable served with butter, cream and a little nutmeg. So is tinned red cabbage with a little extra apple (*see recipe p. .119*). You will also find several ways of using tinned new potatoes (see p. 115–6).

With frozen vegetables you are on to a much safer bet. Good Food Guide inspectors may recognise the difference instantly of course, but luckily the average person (especially if he smokes) usually can't distinguish between a frozen brussel sprout and a fresh one. This goes for most other frozen vegetables except, I should add, the specialised (recipe-type) ones like baby onions in cream sauce (the range is too limited at present for anyone to make extravagant claims of their own about them safely).

If you just want to add them to recipes, dehydrated onions are quite a decent substitute for the real thing and dehydrated peppers and/or mixed vegetables are fine for throwing into rice when its cooking to give it more flavour, or if you're after a good base for a risotto. Instant mashed potato served on its own might, fool a few jaded palates, but unless you're blind as well just its appearance will expose it for what it is. So if you must use it, you'll find a few suggestions on the next page.

Rice is a good way of avoiding vegetables altogether — not simply with curries but with stews and other meat or fish dishes that come with a sauce (see *recipes on p. 122*). Alternatively, many supermarkets and delicatessens serve ready-made salads (coleslaw, Spanish, potato etc.) which will get you out of a jam.

HOW TO HEAVILY DISGUISE INSTANT MASHED POTATO

Most people can spot instant mash a mile off. Not so much, perhaps, by the taste as by the appearance. Here are a few ideas to help you make it look authentic as well as taste good.

1. Make up the mashed potato according to the instructions on the packet and add 2 oz. of cream cheese and 1 oz. of butter that has been melted with a heaped teaspoon of dried chives in it. Beat to mix everything evenly and season well with salt and freshly-milled black pepper.

2. Make up the mashed potato according to the packet instructions and add 2 tablespoons of fresh cream, 1 oz. of butter, 2 oz. of grated Cheddar cheese and lots of fresh-ground salt and pepper.

3. Take a largish onion, chop it small and fry till soft in plenty of butter. Make up the mashed potato and beat the onion and butter into it. Season well.

4. Chop up 2 bunches of spring onions and cook them in 2 oz. of butter for 10 minutes. Make up the instant mash and beat in the onions and butter. Add 2 tablespoons of cream (or top of the milk) and plenty of salt and fresh ground pepper.

✳ Potatoes Lyonnaise   *(serves 4)*

1 1 lb. 3 oz. can of new
  potatoes, drained and
  chopped
Some cooking oil and butter
1 large onion, chopped small

Salt and freshly-milled black
  pepper
1 tablespoon of fresh chopped
  parsley

Drain the potatoes and dry them well in a clean cloth or some kitchen paper. Fry them till crisp in butter and oil. At the same time in another pan, fry the onion in a little butter and oil. To serve, mix the two together and sprinkle salt and pepper and chopped parsley.

❋ Potatoes Niçoise

(serves 4)

1 1 lb. 3 oz. can of new
  potatoes, drained and
  chopped
Some cooking oil and butter
1 large onion, chopped small
1 clove of garlic, minced

1 5 oz. can of red peppers,
  drained and chopped
1 heaped teaspoon of dried
  chives
Salt and freshly-milled pepper

Dry the potatoes in some kitchen paper, then fry them till crisp in some hot oil and butter. Transfer them on to some crumpled kitchen paper and keep warm. Now in the same pan fry the onion, garlic and peppers in more oil and butter. Sprinkle the chives over the potatoes and season well before serving.

❋ Dutch Potatoes

(serves 4)

Some cooking oil
1 1 lb. 3 oz. can of new
  potatoes, drained
1 large onion, chopped small
1 clove of garlic, minced

2 rashers of bacon, chopped
  small
Salt and freshly-milled black
  pepper

Pre-heat oven to 450°F (mark 8)

Put ¼-inch of cooking oil into a roasting tin and pre-heat it in the oven. Meanwhile dry the potatoes thoroughly. When the oil is hot carefully empty the potatoes into it and bake high up in the oven for 20 minutes or until they're golden (turn them once). In the meantime fry the onion, garlic and bacon. Take the potatoes out of the oil with a draining spoon and drain on some kitchen paper. Serve with the bacon and onion sprinkled over with a little seasoning.

❋ New Potatoes with Mint and Chives

(serves 4)

1 1 lb. 3 oz. can of new
  potatoes
2 oz. of butter
1 tablespoon of fresh mint,
  chopped

1 tablespoon of fresh chives,
  or dried, chopped
Salt and freshly-milled black
  pepper

Heat the potatoes as instructed on the tin and drain them well. Melt the butter in a saucepan and add the mint and chives. Then toss the potatoes in the butter and herb mixture until they're well coated. Season to taste and serve.

❋ Buttered Cauliflower with Nutmeg (serves 4–6)

1 large cauliflower
2 bay leaves
½ teaspoon freshly-grated nutmeg

2 oz. of butter
Salt and freshly-milled black pepper

Chop off the hard stalk at the base of the cauliflower but leave on a few of the outer green leaves – they help the flavour. Wash it and have ready in a saucepan, 1-inch of boiling salted water. Pop in a couple of bay leaves, then the cauliflower – base side down – and sprinkle over the top the freshly-grated nutmeg. Cover the saucepan with a well-fitting lid and when you hear the water come back to the boil, turn the heat down to medium and boil for approximately 8 minutes. Test it with a skewer and when it feels cooked (but still firm) drain it and return it to the saucepan with half the butter and some salt and pepper. Shake it for a few minutes and serve it topped with the rest of the butter.

❋ Brussels Sprouts with Chestnuts (serves 4)

1 10 oz. can of unsweetened chestnuts
1 ½ lb. packet of frozen brussels sprouts

2 oz. of butter
Salt and freshly-milled black pepper

Drain the chestnuts and chop them all in half. Cook the sprouts in salted water (for a little less time than it says on the packet). Drain them, then heat the butter and gently sauté the chestnuts in it. Add the sprouts long enough to get them buttery all over. Sprinkle with salt and freshly-milled black pepper and serve.

❋ Spinach with Cream

(serves 2)

- 1 10 oz. packet of frozen chopped spinach
- 2 tablespoons of single cream
- A few gratings of fresh nutmeg
- Salt and freshly-milled black pepper

Cook the spinach according to the instructions on the packet. Drain very thoroughly, pressing to squeeze all the water out. Now put it back into the saucepan, and over a low heat stir the cream into it. Add nutmeg, salt and pepper and serve.

❋ Baked Crumbed Tomatoes

(serves 8)

- 2 heaped tablespoons of packet breadcrumbs
- 2 tablespoons of olive oil
- 1 clove of garlic, crushed
- 1 level teaspoon of dried basil
- ½ teaspoon of thyme
- 8 large tomatoes
- Salt and freshly-milled black pepper

Pre-heat oven to 400°F (mark 6)

Mix the breadcrumbs with the olive oil, garlic and herbs. Cut the tomatoes into halves and place them on a baking sheet. Then place some of the breadcrumb mixture on each half and bake for 20 minutes.

❋ Glazed Carrots

(serves 4)

- 1 15 oz. can of small whole carrots
- 1 tablespoon of caster sugar
- 2 oz. of butter
- Freshly-milled black pepper

Heat the carrots and drain them. Then melt the butter in a saucepan with the sugar and toss the carrots in to cook for about 5 minutes, until they're well glazed. Season with a little black pepper before serving.

❋ Provençale Mushrooms

(serves 4)

- 2 tablespoons of olive oil
- 1 clove of garlic, crushed
- ½ lb. of fresh mushrooms
- Salt and freshly-milled pepper
- 1 tablespoon of fresh parsley, chopped

Heat the oil with the garlic in it in a frying pan, then throw all the mushrooms in (no need to peel or chop them: if they're very dirty just wipe them). Shake the pan and toss the mushrooms around to absorb all the garlic oil, but don't overcook them. Season with salt and pepper and serve with some parsley sprinkled over.

Spiced Red Cabbage (serves 4)

1 14 oz. can of Braised Red Cabbage with Apple (Felix)
2 tablespoons of red wine
1 clove of garlic, crushed
¼ teaspoon of ground cinnamon
Some freshly-grated nutmeg
Freshly-milled black pepper

Put into a saucepan the cabbage with apple, wine, cinnamon, nutmeg, garlic and pepper and allow to simmer very gently for 10 minutes. It's great with all pork dishes.

Ratatouille Provençale (serves 3-4)

1 1 lb. packet of frozen ratatouille Provençale
2 cloves of garlic, crushed
1 teaspoon of olive oil
1 teaspoon of concentrated tomato purée
Salt and freshly-milled black pepper

Heat the ratatouille according to the instructions on the packet and stir in the garlic, tomato purée and olive oil. Season with the salt and pepper. This is a quick way to make chops and steaks more interesting – just spoon the ratatouille over the meat before serving.

Broccoli au Gratin (serves 3-4)

1 oz. of butter
1 9 oz. packet of frozen broccoli
½ packet of white sauce mix
2 oz. of grated Cheddar cheese
½ teaspoon of paprika

Butter a shallow baking dish. Cook the broccoli as it directs on the packet, drain well then arrange it in the baking-dish. Make up the white sauce according to the packet instructions and pour half of it over. Sprinkle the grated cheese on top and place the dish under a hot grill till the cheese begins to brown. Sprinkle with paprika before serving.

SIX QUICK SALADS

✳ Green Salad   (serves 4)

1 bunch of watercress	1 lettuce
1 tablespoon of onion, finely chopped	Vinaigrette dressing (See p. 134)

Don't wash the lettuce because you'll never get it dry again. Just wipe the leaves with a piece of damp kitchen paper. Cut off the tops of the watercress with some scissors and dunk them in cold water, then pat dry in a clean towel. Put all the vegetables, including the onion, into a large salad bowl and pour over just enough dressing to thoroughly coat shortly before serving.

✳ Tomato Salad   (serves 4)

8 large tomatoes	1 heaped tablespoon of onion, finely-chopped
2 heaped tablespoons of parsley, finely-chopped	Vinaigrette dressing (See p. 134)
1 teaspoon of dried basil	

Slice the tomatoes thinly with a sharp knife (don't cut them in quarters). Arrange the slices slightly overlapping on a serving plate, and sprinkle the onion, basil and parsley over them. Pour the dressing on at the last minute and serve with plenty of crusty bread.

✳✳ Health Salad   (serves 4)

1 large dessertspoon of apple, chopped small with skin on	2 medium carrots, grated
1 tablespoon of lemon juice	A handful of currants
½ white cabbage, shredded	2 oz. of walnuts, chopped
2 medium onions, finely chopped	Vinaigrette dressing (see p. 134) or mayonnaise

Toss the apple in the lemon juice to prevent it from dis-colouring. Then mix together the cabbage, the onions, the carrots, the currants and the walnuts. This salad has plenty of staying power and will keep for sometime even when 'dressed'.

❋ Potato Salad   *(serves 4)*

- 1 1 lb. 3 oz. can of new potatoes, well drained
- 1 bunch of spring onions, chopped small
- 1 tablespoon of mint, finely-chopped
- 1 tablespoon of parsley, finely-chopped
- Vinaigrette dressing (See p. 134)

Mix together thoroughly the potatoes, the spring onions, mint, parsley and toss in the dressing. Again, this is a salad which can be made well ahead.

❋ Rice Salad   *(serves 4)*

- 1 dessert apple, finely chopped with the skin on
- ½ lb. of long grain rice, cooked and drained
- 1 5 oz. can of red peppers, drained and chopped
- 1 onion, finely chopped
- 1 tablespoon of parsley, finely chopped
- Vinaigrette dressing (See p. 134)

Toss the apple in a tablespoon of lemon juice to prevent its discolouring. Then add it to the rice, red peppers, onion, parsley and toss it all together evenly with the Vinaigrette dressing.

❋ String Bean Salad   *(serves 4)*

- 1 packet of frozen haricots verts
- Vinaigrette dressing (p. 134)
- 1 tablespoon of spring onions, finely chopped

Cook the beans according to the instructions on the packet, drain and while they're still hot, toss them in the Vinaigrette dressing. Allow them to cool then sprinkle over them the chopped spring onions.

❋❋ Onion Rice   (serves 4)

1 oz. of butter
1 medium onion, chopped small
5 oz. of long grain rice (Uncle Ben's)

Salt and freshly-milled black pepper
2½ cups of hot chicken stock (Knorr Instant)

Melt the butter in a saucepan and gently fry the onion to soften. Add the rice and salt and pepper and stir till it has absorbed all the onion juices and the butter. Now pour in the hot stock, stir once, put a well-fitting lid on the saucepan and cook for 20–25 minutes until all the liquid is absorbed and the rice is cooked.

❋❋ Curry Rice   (serves 4)

1 oz. of butter
1 medium onion, chopped small
5 oz. of long grain rice (Uncle Ben's)
4 whole cloves

1 heaped teaspoon of ground turmeric
Salt and freshly ground black pepper
2½ cups of hot chicken stock (Knorr instant)

Melt the butter and fry the onion gently till softened. Add the rice, turmeric and salt and pepper. Stir till the butter is absorbed. Pour in the stock, stir once, add the cloves and cinnamon and cook with the lid on for 20–25 minutes.

❋❋ Pilaff Rice   (serves 4)

1 medium onion, chopped small
5 oz. of long grain rice (Uncle Ben's)
Salt and freshly-milled black pepper

1 oz. of butter
2 level tablespoons of dehydrated mixed vegetables
2½ cups of hot chicken stock (Knorr instant)

Fry the onion gently in butter till soft, add the rice, and the dehydrated vegetables and stir till the butter is absorbed. Add the hot stock, stir once and cook with the lid on for 20–25 minutes.

List of Recipes

SAUCES

Sauces are what head chefs and Cordon Bleus' usually get very intense about. And they can, it's true, go wrong for the best of cooks. Cheats, though never get bothered. They just make full use of packets and liquidisers and make certain of having whisks and sieves in readiness for extracting lumps.

An infinite variety of sauces can now be bought ready-made at most delicatessens. Even the French classic sauces come in bottles – Escoffier do several including English Cumberland sauce and Sauce Diable. Similarly there are a good many acceptable curry and barbecue sauces, and fortunately you can now buy really authentic tasting Mayonnaise, Bernaise and Hollandaise. However, if either your pocket or your supermarket cannot provide any of these ready-made, the following recipes won't tax your brain or your strength too much, I promise. Always have a good supply of butter, fresh cream and cooking wine handy. All three used together can disguise most instant sauces.

※ Cook-ahead   ✽ Up to 30 mins   ✧ Over 30 mins

SAUCES

❋ Anchovy Sauce

1 packet of white sauce mix
2 dessertspoons of anchovy
  essence
1 dessertspoon of tomato
  ketchup
1 oz. of butter
1 teaspoon of lemon juice
Salt and freshly-milled black
  pepper

Make up the sauce according to the instructions on the packet, then stir in the anchovy essence, ketchup, butter, lemon juice and salt and pepper. This one is particularly good with fresh haddock or halibut, or indeed with most white fish.

❋ Egg Sauce

1 packet of white sauce mix
2 hard boiled eggs, chopped
1 oz. of butter
1 level tablespoon of fresh or
  dried chopped chives
1 tablespoon of cream, or top
  of the milk
Salt and freshly-milled black
  pepper

Make up the white sauce according to the directions on the packet, stir in the eggs, butter and cream, then season to taste. Add the chives and serve with poached fish or, best of all, smoked haddock.

❋ Lemon Sauce

1 packet of white sauce mix
Grated peel of 1 lemon
Juice of 1 lemon
1 oz. of butter
A little single cream
Salt and freshly-milled black
  pepper

Make up the white sauce according to the directions on the packet, add the lemon peel and juice. Over a very low heat stir the sauce and let it absorb the lemon flavour for 5 minutes. Just before serving, stir in the butter and a little cream, and let them melt. Season to taste and serve with poached fish or boiled chicken.

✢ Mustard Sauce

1 packet of white sauce mix
2 level tablespoons of dry English mustard
1 oz. of butter

3 level tablespoons of single cream, or top of the milk
Salt and freshly-milled black pepper

Make up the white sauce according to the packet instructions. Mix the mustard with the cream making sure it's smooth and free from lumps. Add it to the sauce and melt some butter in it. Season to taste and serve with fried or grilled herrings or mackerel.

✢ Cheese Sauce

1 packet of cheese sauce mix
2 oz. of grated Cheddar cheese
1 tablespoon of grated Parmesan cheese

¼ teaspoon of dried mustard
1 oz. of butter
Salt and freshly-milled black pepper

Make up the cheese sauce according to the instructions on the packet, then add the other cheeses. Sprinkle in the mustard and add the butter. Stir till the butter is melted, season to taste and serve with eggs, cauliflower, leeks or baked fish.

✢ Onion Sauce

1 packet of onion sauce mix
1 bay leaf
2 oz. of butter
1 medium onion, chopped small
Salt and milled black pepper

2 pinches of ground cloves
Freshly grated nutmeg
1 tablespoon of cream, or top of the milk

Make up the sauce according to the instructions on the packet, adding a bay leaf. In another saucepan melt the butter and gently fry the onion in it, without letting it brown (10–15 minutes). Add the onion and the butter it was cooked in to the sauce. Season with salt and pepper and add the powdered cloves and a few grating of nutmeg. Just before serving stir in the cream. Serve with roast lamb, boiled ham or vegetables like cauliflower or broccoli.

✲ Parsley Sauce

1 packet of parsley sauce mix
2 tablespoons of parsley, freshly chopped
2 tablespoons of single cream
Salt and freshly-milled black pepper

When you've made the sauce according to the directions on the packet, add the chopped parsley and cream to it and stir. Season to your taste and serve with poached or baked fish or boiled bacon.

✲ Mornay Sauce

1 packet of white sauce mix
2 tablespoons of grated Gruyère cheese, or Emmenthal
1 oz. of butter
2 tablespoons of grated Parmesan
Salt and freshly-milled black pepper
2 tablespoons of single cream

Make up the sauce mix according to the directions on the packet, then over a low heat stir in the two cheeses and the butter (the cheese will take 5 or 6 minutes to melt). Season with salt and pepper and add the cream. This can be served with chicken, fish or vegetables.

◍ Blender Hollandaise

4 oz. of butter
2 egg yolks
2 tablespoons of lemon juice
Salt and milled black pepper

In a small saucepan gently heat the butter until it begins to foam. Put the 2 egg yolks and lemon juice into the liquidiser goblet with some salt and pepper. Place the lid on the goblet and blend on a high speed for a few seconds. Then remove the cap and pour in the melted butter in a steady stream with the motor running. When all the butter has been added, switch off, pour out and serve while still warm. Don't attempt to reheat the Hollandaise — because it will separate.

This buttery sauce is delicious with asparagus, poached and baked white fish, baked salmon, steaks or chops.

⚘ Sauce Bernaise

2 tablespoons of dry white wine
1 tablespoon of wine vinegar
1 teaspoon of dried tarragon
1 tablespoon of onion, finely chopped
Ingredients as for Hollandaise sauce

Put the wine, vinegar, tarragon and onion in a small saucepan. Bring to the boil and continue until the liquid is reduced by half. Now pour it into the Hollandaise sauce (see recipe above) in the blender and blend for a few seconds on high speed. Serve with steak, roast beef or fish.

Mint Bernaise

Follow the recipe above using 1 teaspoon of dried mint in place of tarragon. Serve with roast lamb or lamb chops.

❋ Spiced Barbecue Sauce

3 tablespoons of malt vinegar
1 teaspoon of dried mustard
1 tablespoon of Worcester-shire sauce
2 teaspoons of Tabasco sauce
1 teaspoon of salt
2 tablespoons of soft brown sugar
1 level teaspoon of powdered ginger
1 medium onion, chopped very small

Put everything into a saucepan and bring to simmering point, stirring continuously with a wooden spoon. Then let it simmer gently for about 15 minutes. Use the sauce for basting roast chicken, pork, or spare ribs.

❋ Spiced Apple Sauce

1 7½ oz. can of apple sauce (Hero)
¼ teaspoon of ground cloves
A little grated nutmeg
¼ teaspoon of ground cinnamon
1 tablespoon of cider

Mix the apple sauce, cloves, cinnamon, nutmeg and cider together and heat gently. Serve with roast pork or pork chops.

✳ Mushroom Sauce /1

1 10 oz. can of condensed mushroom soup
¼ pint of milk
Freshly-milled black pepper

1 7½ oz. can of grilling mushrooms, drained and chopped
2 tablespoons of single cream

Gently heat the soup thinned with the milk and stir in the mushrooms. Season with pepper and just before serving, stir in the cream. Delicious with baked fish or chicken.

✳ Mushroom Sauce /2

1 packet of instant mushroom sauce
¼ lb. of fresh mushrooms, thinly sliced

2 oz. of butter
Salt and freshly-milled black pepper

Make up the sauce as on the packet, then melt the butter in a frying pan. Throw in the sliced mushrooms and toss them in the butter for a few minutes. Add them to the sauce and season with salt and pepper.

✳✳ Gooseberry Sauce

1 15 oz. can of gooseberries
Salt and freshly-milled black pepper

A little grated nutmeg
1 oz. of butter

Simply blend the contents of the can of gooseberries in the liquidiser for a few seconds, adding a little salt and pepper and a few gratings of nutmeg. Heat it gently with a knob of butter and serve it over grilled or fried mackerel.

❋ Orange Sauce

The grated rind of 1 small orange	1 heaped teaspoon of arrowroot
⅓ pint of fresh orange juice	A little water
1½ oz. of sugar	1 11 oz. can of mandarin oranges, drained
A little salt	

Blanch the orange rind by boiling it in water for 10 minutes. Drain well and add to it the orange juice and sugar, and bring to simmering point. Thicken it with arrowroot mixed with a little water, and a little salt added. Now add the drained mandarins. Let them heat through then serve with roast duck (and it's good with roast chicken too).

❋ Cherry Sauce

½ 5 oz. jar of Morello cherry jam	¼ pint of red wine
	Salt and freshly-milled pepper

Please make a note that it's essential to use *Morello* cherry jam for this – no other sort of jam will do as well.

Simply heat up the jam and wine with a little seasoning and let it simmer gently for about 10 minutes. This cherry sauce is the very nicest thing to serve with duck.

❋ Bread Sauce

Believe me, I've tried very hard to get instant bread sauce that's remotely like the real thing, and I've failed miserably. Real bread sauce should be creamy and buttery – not like a tasteless lump of porridge. So I'm using a non-cheating recipe here, but it's dead simple if you make the breadcrumbs in the liquidiser.

1 medium onion	3 oz. of fresh white breadcrumbs
Whole cloves	
¾ pint of milk	1 tablespoon of single cream
1 bay leaf	Salt and freshly-milled black pepper
2 oz. of butter	

First peel the onion and cut in half. Stick cloves into the 2 halves (I use about 15 but you can use less if you want to).

Put the onion halves into the milk in a saucepan, throw in a bay leaf and heat it gently (but not anywhere near boiling-point). Then leave it in a warm place for a couple of hours. At the end of that time, re-heat it very, very slowly for about 15 minutes until it reaches boiling-point. Lift out the onion and bay leaf (but keep them by), stir in the bread-crumbs and half the butter. Leave it on a very low heat for about 10 minutes till the breadcrumbs have swollen up. Now pop the onion back in and leave it in a warm place till you're ready to serve. Before serving, however, discard the onion, beat in the remaining butter and the cream, and taste to check the seasoning.

COLD SAUCES

MAYONNAISE SAUCES

For all three sauces it's essential to buy an authentic mayonnaise. There are several brands available in high-class grocers, health-food shops and delicatessens. So it's up to you to find one you like.

✻✻ Aiöli (garlic mayonnaise)

6 oz. of mayonnaise
3 cloves of garlic, crushed
Salt and milled black pepper

Mix the mayonnaise, garlic and seasoning several hours before you need it. It goes very well with prawns, cold flaked fish and grilled steaks and chops (*but* only if you like garlic).

✻ Green Mayonnaise

6 oz. of mayonnaise
2 tablespoons of parsley, finely chopped
2 tablespoons of watercress, finely chopped
Salt and milled black pepper

Blend together the mayonnaise, parsley, watercress and seasoning not too long before you need it (because it tends to discolour). Serve it with cold salmon (fresh or tinned).

✳✳ Remoulade Sauce

6 oz. of mayonnaise
1 tablespoon of capers
2 tablespoons of pickled
cucumbers, chopped small
1 level teaspoon of dried
English mustard

1 tablespoon of parsley,
finely chopped
1 level teaspoon of tarragon
Salt and freshly-milled black
pepper

Thoroughly mix together the mayonnaise, capers, pickled cucumbers, mustard, parsley, tarragon and season to taste. Serve with fried fish and sea food. And it does wonders for good old fish fingers!

✳✳ Tartare Sauce

4 heaped tablespoons of
bought tartare sauce
1 tablespoon of chopped
capers, drained

4 small sweet gherkins,
chopped
1 clove of garlic, crushed

Mix the tartare sauce, chopped capers, gherkins and garlic evenly together and serve with fried fish or shellfish.

✳✳ Cumberland Sauce

2 tablespoons of redcurrant
jelly
2 tablespoons of port
1 heaped teaspoon of dried
English mustard
1 heaped teaspoon of
powdered ginger.

Juice of 1 small orange
Juice of a ½ lemon
Grated peel of 1 small orange
Grated rind of 1 lemon
Salt and freshly-milled black
pepper

Melt the redcurrant jelly with the port over a low heat – about 15 minutes. Then mix the mustard and ginger smoothly with the orange and lemon juice. Boil the orange and lemon peel in water for 5 minutes to remove any bitterness, then combine everything, giving it all a good whisk and season to taste. Serve this sauce with cold ham, hot boiled or baked ham, roast duck. This sauce is always served cold, even if it accompanies something hot.

❋❋ Spring Sauce for Lamb

2 tablespoons of mint, freshly chopped

2 tablespoons of spring onions, very finely chopped

2 tablespoons of lettuce, finely shredded

8 fl. oz. of malt vinegar

1 level teaspoon of sugar

Toss the mint, onions, lettuce, vinegar and sugar lightly together in a bowl and serve with roast lamb in the spring and summer.

❋❋ Vinaigrette Dressing   (serves 4–6)

(Of course, you can buy dressings in assorted flavours but it's so easy to make this one yourself)

2 tablespoons of wine vinegar

1 level teaspoon of salt

1 level teaspoon of freshly milled black pepper

10 tablespoons of olive oil

1 level teaspoon of dried mustard

1 clove of garlic, crushed (optional)

In a small jug put the vinegar and seasoning and leave it for an hour or longer so that the salt can dissolve. Pour in the oil, and then the whole mixture into a screwtop jar or bottle – and shake like mad to blend it evenly. Store it in the bottle and shake again before using.

List of Recipes

LIST OF RECIPES

DESSERTS

When you're entertaining and pondering over a sweet course don't be put off by the dedicated dieters. They might be great martyrs to the cause when they're at home, but in their heart of hearts they're just dying for something exotic when they're being entertained, which politeness 'forces' them to accept. 'How on earth can I refuse that, when you've worked so hard?' they say. Well, in this chapter we're not *going* to work very hard, thank you. But we *are* going to produce the most irresistible desserts.

Whether you're an experienced cook or a beginner at cheating, the one thing that matters most when it comes to puddings is imagination. Supermarkets can't provide you with that, but their shelves are positively bulging with aids: instant chocolate sauces, melba sauces, crumble toppings, fruit pie fillings, unusual tinned fruits that just need a little liqueur added or frozen mousses that with a few subtle additions will fool everyone. And when your imagination seems to have deserted you, look around for (and keep stocked in your kitchen) ever-readies like a can of Crème

※ Cook-ahead ❉ Up to 30 mins ◈ Over 30 mins

de marron: topped with some fresh cream it'll provide you with a sure-fire success in as short a time as it takes to get off the lid. Experiment with ice-creams, which now come in large 'serve-again' packs and in flavours that range from peppermint to Marsala, and with the spirits you perhaps brought back from your foreign holiday (brandy is the great stand-by, but rum, coffee liqueur and cooking sherry will also do nicely). Among the accessories you'll be glad to have around in a crisis I'd list: toasted almonds, nibbed nuts, toasted hazelnuts, fan-shaped wafers and boudoir biscuits, a supply of instant custard, fresh cream, bars of plain chocolate and Digestive biscuits

❋ Banana Butterscotch Pudding (serves 4)

1 packet of Butterscotch Instant Whip
4 bananas, peeled and sliced

4 Digestive biscuits, crushed into crumbs
4 teaspoons of nibbed nuts

Mix the instant whip according to the instructions on the packet. Stir it into the bananas and biscuit crumbs. Divide into 4 servings and top each one with nibbed nuts.

❋ One-minute Banana Dessert (serves 4)

6 bananas, peeled and sliced
4 tablespoons of bramble jelly

4 tablespoons of fresh single cream

Put the bananas into 4 fruit bowls and top with bramble jelly and cream.

❋ Fruit Salad Exotica (serves 6)

1 15 oz. can of figs in syrup
1 15 oz. can of guavas in syrup
1 15 oz. can of lychees in syrup
1 11 oz. can of loganberries

1 15 oz. can of mangoes in syrup
Pernod, or Cointreau of Cognac

Mix together the figs, guavas, lychees, mangoes and loganberries, pour over a little Pernod (not *too* much as a little goes a long way!). Chill and serve.

❊ Brandied Plums   *(serves 4)*

Tip out a 15 oz. can of plums into a bowl and pour over the fruit as much brandy as you can spare. Chill and serve with whipped cream.

❊ Cardinal Peaches   *(serves 4)*

Drain a 15 oz can of peach halves, then into fruit dishes put first a blob of vanilla ice-cream, then 2 peach halves. Cover with an instant melba sauce. Top with whipped cream and serve with crunchy wafer biscuits.

❊ Chocolate Nut Sundae   *(serves 4)*

Half-fill 4 dessert glasses with vanilla ice-cream. Pour over each some instant chocolate sauce and top with a blob of whipped cream and toasted almonds.

❊ Coffee Ice   *(serves 4)*

Scoop some coffee ice-cream into 4 bowls, pour over each portion some coffee liqueur and sprinkle with chopped nuts.

❊ Mont Blanc   *(serves 4)*

1 8 oz. can of creme de marron, sweetened chestnut purée
4 cream-filled meringues, from a shop
1 small block of vanilla ice
¼ pint of double cream, whipped

In four fruit dishes put first a tablespoon of marron, then divide the meringues into halves and press them into the marron, leaving a gap in the middle (this can be done well in advance). To serve, fill the gaps between the meringues with ice-cream and cover with whipped cream. And try to remember not to give it to anyone who's on a diet.

❊ Apple Fool   *(serves 4)*

Mix 1 14½ oz. can of apple pie filling with 2 5 oz. cartons of yoghurt and chill.

❄ Gooseberry Fool (serves 4)

1 15 oz. can of gooseberries, well drained

½ pint of double cream, whipped

Blend the gooseberries to a pulp in the liquidiser. Empty the purée into a bowl containing the whipped cream. Fold the gooseberry pulp into the cream blending thoroughly. Pour into tall glasses and chill for 2 to 3 hours. Serve just as it is.

❄ Rhubarb Fool (serves 4)

1 11 oz. can of rhubarb, well drained

1 dessertspoon of lemon juice (instant)

½ teaspoon of powdered ginger

½ pint of double cream, whipped

Blend the rhubarb, lemon juice and ginger in the liquidiser, then mix the resulting purée with the whipped cream, making sure it's all evenly mixed. Pour into glasses and chill thoroughly before serving.

❄ Fresh Strawberry Fool (serves 4)

1 lb. of strawberries, washed and hulled

2 oz. of caster sugar

½ pint of double cream, whipped

Reserve four huge strawberries to decorate at the end. Blend the rest of the strawberries in the liquidiser in two or three lots, adding the sugar. Then mix the resulting purée with the whipped cream. Pour into glasses and chill thoroughly. Serve with a strawberry popped on top of each helping.

❄ Orange and Apricot Cream (serves 4)

1 14½ oz. can of apricot pie filling

1 tablespoon of lemon juice

1 11 oz. can of mandarin oranges, drained

The grated rind of 1 orange

¼ pint of double cream, whipped

2 tablespoons of flaked toasted almonds

Put the contents of the can of pie filling into the liquidiser with the lemon juice and blend till you have a smooth purée. Empty the purée into a bowl and blend it with the whipped cream. Stir in half the oranges, then pour the mixture into tall-stemmed glasses. Decorate with the rest of the oranges and sprinkle over the toasted almonds. Serve thoroughly chilled.

❋ Chocolate Orange Mousse   (serves 4)

6 2 oz. portions of frozen
  chocolate mousse, thawed
The grated rind of 1 small
  orange
1 tablespoon of fresh orange
  juice

2 tablespoons of dark rum
4 heaped teaspoons of whipped
  double cream
1 tablespoon of plain chocolate, grated

In a basin mix the four mousses together and add the grated orange peel, juice and rum. Now divide the mousses into four little pots or glasses and let them chill thoroughly in the refrigerator. Before serving, put a teaspoon of whipped cream on to each one and sprinkle grated chocolate over. Serve with boudoir biscuits.

❋ Iced Lemon Mousse   (serves 4)

6 2 oz. portions frozen lemon
  mousse, thawed
The grated rind of 2 lemons
1 tablespoon of lemon juice

¼ pint of double cream,
  whipped
A few chilled white grapes,
  halved and de-pipped

Mix the mousses together with the grated lemon peel and juice, and fold in half the whipped cream. Pile the mousse into four tall-stemmed wine glasses and chill thoroughly. Serve topped with the rest of the whipped cream and decorate with the grape halves.

✳ Ten-minute Trifle   *(serves 4)*

½ Swiss roll, sliced
4 tablespoons of sherry
1 11 oz. can of mandarin
  oranges, drained
3 bananas

1 15 oz. can of ready-made
  custard
½ pint of extra thick cream
Nibbed nuts

Take four tallish dessert glasses and into them put the slices of Swiss roll. Pour over the sherry and agitate with a spoon until it has soaked into the sponge. Now put in the oranges, the bananas and the custard in that order. Finally, a huge blob of thick cream and lots of nibbed nuts. Chill before serving.

✳ Cherry Flan   *(serves 4)*

2 tablespoons of sherry
1 ready-made sponge flan-case

1 14½ oz. can of cherry pie
  filling

Sprinkle the sherry into the sponge base and empty the cherry filling in to the centre and spread evenly.

✳ Fruit Tart   *(serves 4)*

6 oz. of self-raising flour
3 oz. of butter
1½ lb. of sliced apples *or*
1½ lb. of fresh apricots
  stoned and halved

2 tablespoons of caster sugar
1 large egg
1 separate dessertspoon of
  caster sugar

Pre-heat oven to 350°F (mark 4)

Take a large mixing bowl and seive the flour into it. Cut the butter into small pieces and rub it into the flour using your finger tips and lifting it to get the air in. When all the flour and butter is rubbed together (it will look crumbly) add the sugar and then break the egg into a cup. Mix it with a fork and add it to the mixture. Using the fork, mix the egg in well. Flour your hands and knead the mixture to form a soft dough. If it seems too dry, just add a little drop of milk. Now transfer the pastry on to a well greased shallow (oblong) baking tin and press it down with your hands to form a flat (oblong) base. Lightly place the apricot halves, or apple slices all over the base (place the apricots with their rounded side uppermost). Sprinkle the dessertspoon of caster sugar all over the top and bake in the upper part of the oven for 45 minutes. Serve with cream. This is nicest when eaten as fresh as possible.

Apricot Crumble   (serves 4)

1 14½ oz. can of apricot pie filling
2 level teaspoons of ground cinnamon

2 6 oz. packets of ready-made crumble mix
2 level dessertspoons of soft brown sugar

Pre-heat oven to 400°F (mark 6)

Grease a pie-dish, put in first the apricots filling then sprinkle in 1 teaspoon of ground cinnamon. In a basin, fork the crumble mixture into fine crumbs, pour it evenly over the fruit and top it with the brown sugar and another teaspoon of ground cinnamon. Bake for 40 minutes.

Spiced Apple Crumble   (serves 4)

1½ lb. of cooking apples, peeled cored and sliced
4 tablespoons of water
3 oz. of sugar
1½ teaspoons of ground cinnamon

4 cloves
2 6 oz. packets of ready-made crumble
2 tablespoons of soft brown sugar

Pre-heat oven to 400°F (mark 6)

Grease a pie-dish and put the apples in covered with the water and sugar. Sprinkle in 1 teaspoon of ground cinnamon and place a clove here and there. Break up the crumble mixture with a fork and sprinkle it over the apples. Top with ½ a teaspoon of cinnamon and the brown sugar. Bake for 40 minutes.

✿ Mincemeat and Apple Crumble   *(serves 4)*

1 14½ oz. can of apple pie filling

3 tablespoons of sweet mincemeat

1 packet of ready-made crumble topping

2 tablespoons of soft brown sugar

Pre-heat oven to 400°F (mark 6)

Grease a pie-dish and put in the apple pie filling and mincemeat (mixing it a bit with a fork). Crumble the topping with a fork and spread it over the fruit. Sprinkle brown sugar on top and bake for 40 minutes till the top is golden brown and crunchy.

✿ Rhubarb Crumble   *(serves 4)*

1½ lb. of rhubarb, washed and cut in chunks

2–3 tablespoons of water

2 level teaspoons of powdered ginger

2 6 oz. packets of ready-made crumble

3 oz. of caster sugar

2 tablespoons of soft brown sugar

Pre-heat oven to 400°F (mark 6)

Grease a pie-dish and put the rhubarb in it with 2 or 3 tablespoons of water and a teaspoon of ginger sprinkled over. Put it in the oven to cook a little (about 15 minutes). Then lift it out and sprinkle the crumble topping on with another level teaspoon of powdered ginger and 2 tablespoons of soft brown sugar. Bake it for 40 minutes.

How to avoid making pastry

Well, to start with you can always go out and buy some ready-made, fresh or frozen – and very good it is too. Only a dedicated expert would be able to tell the difference between bought and homemade pastry (especially when it has other flavours with it). But if you don't have the time to go out, or wait for it to thaw or whatever, here's what to do:

First make sure your store cupboard is never without plain digestive biscuits, and for what we want them for, it doesn't really matter if they're stale. Here is the recipe for a *Digestive Crumb Crust* for flans, pies or anything that needs a pastry base. To line an 8-inch flan tin or pie-dish you will need:

8 digestive biscuits
2 oz. of butter

Lay the biscuits out flat on a pastry board or working surface, then crush them with a rolling-pin or milk bottle. It's the easiest thing in the world and won't take more than a couple of minutes. (Alternatively, pop them into the blender for a few seconds. This saves even more time and cleaning up.) Now put the crumbs into a mixing bowl, gently melt the butter without letting it brown, and stir it into the crumbs. Then empty the crumb mixture into a flan tin or pie-dish, and press it all down flat, rather like a wall-to-wall carpet. You can press it up slightly round the sides as well. That's it. Now all you have to do is chill it for three hours in the fridge, or bake it on 375°F (mark 5) for 15 minutes.

Many of the following recipes, which once needed pastry, are equally delicious with this crumb crust instead.

✥ Viennese Coffee Flan   *(serves 4)*

2 5 fl. oz. cartons of coffee cream dessert (available in most supermarkets, usually alongside the yoghurts)
2 tablespoons of Tia Maria (coffee liqueur)
1 5 fl. oz. carton of double cream
1 dessertspoon of caster sugar
1 tablespoon of instant coffee
2 tablespoons of hot water
1 8-inch flan tin lined with crumb crust
1 chocolate flake bar (broken up)

Stir the coffee desserts with the liqueur (if you haven't got it brandy or rum will do). Spread it evenly over the crumb base and chill for one to 3 hours. Whip the cream with a dessertspoon of caster sugar, and add to it 1 tablespoon of instant coffee mixed with 2 tablespoons of hot water (allow to cool a bit first). Spread the coffee cream mixture over the flan and decorate with the broken-up chocolate flake.

◑ Jamaican Chocolate Almond Pie   (serves 4)

4 2 oz. portions of frozen
chocolate mousse, thawed

4 tablespoons of dark rum

2 oz. of plain chocolate,
grated

2 oz. of toasted flaked almonds

1 8-inch flan tin lined with
crumb crust

¼ pint of double cream,
whipped

In a mixing bowl, mix the chocolate mousses with half the
rum, half the grated chocolate and half the toasted almonds.
Pour the mixture on to the crumb crust, spread it evenly
and chill for 3 hours (preferably – but 1 hour should do
it). Before serving, mix the cream with the other half of the
rum, spread it over the pie and decorate with the rest of
the grated chocolate and toasted almonds.

❊ Summer Fruit Flan   (serves 4)

¼ lb. of strawberries, hulled
and washed

¼ lb. of raspberries, washed

¾-lb. of redcurrants, picked
and washed

1 8-inch pie dish, lined with
crumb crust

5 fl. oz. carton of double
cream, whipped

Caster sugar

Prepare the fruit and chill it well. Have the crumb crust
well-chilled too. Spread the whipped double cream evenly
over the bottom and just before serving pile the fruit on top
of the cream. Have some caster sugar on the table to pass
around.

◑ Farmhouse Treacle Tart   (serves 4)

1 8-inch pie dish lined with
crumb crust

3 heaped tablespoons of fresh
breadcrumbs (made in
liquidiser)

The juice of ½ the lemon

Grated peel of 1 small lemon

2 tablespoons of golden syrup,
warmed

¼ teaspoon of powdered
ginger

Pre-heat oven to 350°F (mark 4)

Mix the breadcrumbs with the warmed treacle, lemon juice,
peel and powdered ginger. Pour the mixture over the crumb
base and bake in the oven for 35–40 minutes.

✳ Mince Pies   *(serves 8–10)*

- 1 lb. of bought mince meat
- 2 tablespoons of brandy
- The grated peel of 1 small orange
- The grated peel of 1 small lemon
- ¼ nutmeg, grated
- ¾ lb. of frozen shortcrust pastry, thawed
- A little milk
- Sifted icing sugar

Pre-heat oven to 425°F (mark 7)

Mix the mincemeat with the lemon and orange peel and stir in the grated nutmeg and brandy. Mix very thoroughly so that all the flavours are evenly distributed. Now roll out the pastry to about 1/8 inch thick, and cut half of it into 3 inch rounds and half into 2½ inch rounds (rolling up the scraps and repeating till you run out of pastry). Grease the pastry tins lightly and line them with the larger rounds. Fill them with the mincemeat (but not too much, only to the level of the edges of the pastry). Now damp the smaller rounds of pastry with water and press them lightly in position to form lids. Brush them with milk and make a couple of nips in each one with scissors. Bake highish in the oven for 15–20 minutes until light golden brown. Cool on a wire rack and sprinkle with sieved icing sugar. Store in a tin and warm slightly before serving.

◍ Bilberry Cheesecake   *(serves 6)*

- 12 oz. of cream cheese
- 2 eggs
- 2 tablespoons of caster sugar
- 3 drops of vanilla essence
- 1 8-inch flan tin lined with crumb crust
- 1 5 fl. oz. carton of soured cream
- 1 teaspoon of caster sugar
- 1 14½ oz. can of Bilberry pie filling
- 2 tablespoons of extra Digestive crumbs

Pre-heat oven to 350°F (mark 4)

Put the cream cheese, eggs and sugar into a large mixing-bowl. Start mixing with a fork for a bit, then blend till smooth with an electric mixer or rotary whisk. Add three drops of vanilla essence and pour the mixture into the crumb base. Bake for 30 minutes or until the centre feels firm. Now turn up the heat to 450°F (mark 8). Spread the soured cream over, sprinkle on 1 teaspoon of caster sugar and let it bake for another 5 minutes (it goes by very quickly, so don't go away). Allow it to cool, then chill it in the fridge very thoroughly. Turn the cheesecake upside down on to a plate, then right way up on to another. Spread the bilberry filling over the top of the cake and press the extra biscuits crumbs firmly all round the sides.

Everyone will beg you for the recipe, but you can easily put them off by telling them how difficult bilberries are to get hold of and how the cheesecake takes *simply* hours to prepare.

✻ Black Forest Gâteau *(serves 4)*

- 1 15 oz. can of black cherries, drained
- 2 tablespoons of brandy
- 1 frozen chocolate fresh cream sponge
- 2 tablespoons of instant chocolate sauce
- 5 fl. oz. carton of fresh double cream, whipped
- 2 oz. of grated plain chocolate

First of all, mix the cherries with 2 tablespoons of brandy and leave them to soak in it for an hour. Split the sponge open with a sharp knife while it's still frozen. Spread the chocolate sauce over the half that has the least cream on it. Now arrange the cherries on the half that does have the cream on it (reserving a few for later) and put the other half on top pressing lightly. Now take a palette knife and spread the whipped cream all over – down the sides as well. Finish off by pressing grated chocolate into the sides and sprinkling it all over the top. Decorate with the rest of the cherries. Leave in a cool place till the cake is thawed.

✻ Raspberry Gâteau *(serves 4)*

Drain an 11 oz. can of raspberries. Reserve a few and sandwich the rest in between a frozen fresh cream sponge (thawed, of course). Spread whipped cream over the top of the sponge and decorate with a few raspberries.

❄ Apple Crumble Cake   (serves 4)

- 1 packet of Victoria Sponge mix (Lyons)
- 1 large cooking apple, peeled, cored and thinly sliced
- 1 6 oz. packet of ready-made crumble
- 2 tablespoons of soft brown sugar
- 1 teaspoon of ground cinnamon

Pre-heat oven to 400°F (mark 6)

Butter an 8-inch cake tin (with a false bottom) and dust it with flour. Make up the sponge mix according to the directions on the packet. Spoon it on to the cake tin and spread it out evenly. Now lay the apple slices lightly all over the sponge mix. Next sprinkle the crumble all over and top it with brown sugar and cinnamon. Bake it for about a ½ hour and allow to cool before turning out.

◈ Chocolate Fudge Cake   (serves 6)

- ¼ lb. of plain chocolate
- 2 tablespoons of rum
- 1 oz. of butter
- 1 level dessertspoon of instant coffee
- 1 egg
- ¼ pint double cream, whipped
- 2 oz. of walnuts, chopped small
- ½ lb. of Digestive biscuits, crushed into crumbs
- 1 oz. of plain chocolate, grated

Pre-heat oven to 300°F (mark 2)

Break up the chocolate and put it in a basin with the rum. Place the basin in the oven to melt the chocolate for about 15 minutes. Then remove it from the oven, toss in the butter and instant coffee, then with a wooden spoon mix it till smooth. Let it cool a bit before adding the beaten egg and about 1 tablespoon of the whipped cream. Blend thoroughly, then stir in the nuts and biscuits. Put the mixture into an 8-inch cake tin lined with cooking foil. Let it chill through (3 to 4 hours) and serve it with the rest of the cream spread over and sprinkled with grated chocolate.

✻ Shortcut Christmas cake

Buy a Christmas cake (without icing) about 2 weeks before Christmas. It's essential to get one from a reliable baker (or if you can get hold of a Marks & Spencer's or Harrods' variety, all to the good; the latter you can buy by post). Now to start with you need a thin skewer and a miniature bottle of brandy. When you first buy the cake, make some tiny holes in the top with the skewer – dig deep down – and pour drops of brandy into the holes. After 2 or 3 days do the same thing on the underneath of the cake. Keep repeating this every few days, until you run out of brandy.

If you want to ice the cake, buy some ready-made almond paste. For a 9-inch cake you'll need about 2 lb. Roll it out on a board sprinkled with icing sugar and measure and cut a round piece for the top and a long strip for the side. Brush the cake with some sieved apricot jam and stick the almond paste to it – side piece first, then the top. Leave it like that for 3 days.

✻ Shortcut icing

2 lb. of icing sugar, sifted   3 egg whites

Get a large mixing bowl and put the egg whites into it. Beat in the icing sugar a little at a time (an electric mixer at medium speed is very handy for this) until the mixture is smooth and thick enough to stand up in peaks when you pull it up with a spoon. If it's too dry add a little more egg white. Before you start to ice the cake put a spoonful of your icing mixture on to a suitably-sized cake board, centre the cake on it and press it down gently but firmly. Now using a palette knife scrape all the icing out of the bowl on to the waiting Christmas cake and spread it all over the top and down the sides. Go on spreading till there are no dark patches of cake peeping through anywhere. Now move your palette knife down, then draw it up bringing the icing into small peaks. Do this top and sides till the cake resembles a Christmas snow scene. Leave it to set and store in a tin till needed.

✿ Brandy Butter (serves 6–8)

4 oz. of unsalted butter
8 oz. of caster sugar

3 or 4 tablespoons of brandy

Make sure you take the butter out of the fridge well before
you need it, so it's not too hard. Take a largish bowl and
a wooden spoon and beat the butter till it's creamy. Add
the sugar, a teaspoonful at a time, beating furiously. When
all the sugar is in, and it's light and fluffy, start adding the
brandy a drop at a time (about a ½ teaspoon). Beat well
after each addition of brandy to stop it curdling. When all
the brandy is in, pile it into a serving bowl and keep in the
fridge or a cool place. This is excellent served with
Plum pudding (Harrod's).

✿ Spiced Rum Butter (serves 6-8)

4 oz. of butter
4 oz. of soft brown sugar
¼ teaspoon of ground cin-
namon

4 tablespoons of rum
¼ nutmeg, grated
¼ teaspoon of grated lemon
rind

Proceed exactly as for brandy butter (above) adding the
spices and lemon rind last. This makes a nice alternative
to the more usual Brandy Butter and is excellent with hot
Mince pies.

SOME MENUS

Recommended wines are set in *italic* next to the appropriate course. (See the Index for recipes.)

SEDUCTION SCENE: where it's just you and him. You want to prove you can cook (or at the very least, are keen to please), but just as important you want to leave yourself maximum time with him rather than in the kitchen (where, if you stay too long, he's sure to follow you).

Salmon mousse with
    cucumber soured cream   *Alsatian Reisling 1969 (Hugel)*
Mustard-glazed lamb chops   *Pradel Rosé (Provence)*
Ratatouille, Provençale mushrooms
Gooseberry fool   *No wine or Champagne all the way*
                        through – Pommery & Greno 1969

FOREIGN RELATIONS: your friends are over from France or America or wherever and are convinced the English only eat fish and chips.

Cucumber soup
Lancashire Hotpot *Hermitage Rouge 1962 (Nicolas)*
Spiced red cabbage
Farmhouse treacle tart

WITHOUT WARNING: suddenly, and with time for you only
to dash to the late supermarket, he brings the boss home for
what he calls a 'quick snack' and bosses *never* eat quick
snacks, do they?

Consommé *Harvey's Bristol Fino*
Florentine plaice fillets *Muscadet-de-Sèvre et Maine Château*
de la Cassemichère 1969

Green salad
Mont Blanc

GOOD IMPRESSIONS: the moment you've dreaded, perhaps.
Mother-in-law is coming to dinner determined to prove
what a layabout is looking after her son.

Avocado soup
Trout with almong butter *Meursault 1963 (Louis Jadot)*
New potatoes with chives
Salad
Viennese coffee flan

ANNIVERSARY: the day he'll want his favourite food, but
he's always so vague about what he likes best. So, you've
just got to make it happy and colourful.

Prawn pâté *Muscadet (Mottron)*
Spiced chicken *Tavel Rosé (Moreau-Fontaine)*
Curry rice
Cardinal peaches *Château Climens 1964*

FOR AN OUTING: it's a lovely day. Your friends have rung
up and said 'Let's go for a picnic — we'll bring the booze,
if you make the food'. They'll want more than sandwiches.

Cold meat loaf *Goldener Oktober Moselle*
Rice salad
Health salad
Apple crumble cake

WINTER
January
Leek and potato soup
Stuffed pork chops *Moulin à Vent 1968 (Moreau Fontaine)*
Spiced red cabbage
Orange and apricot cream

February
French onion soup
Beef Goulash *Châteauneuf du Pape 1968 Moreau Fontaine)*
Mashed potato with onion
Brussels sprouts with chestnuts
Fruit salad exotica

March
Spiced grapefruit
Sole Veronique
   with iced grapes *Alsatian Riesling 1969 (Hugel)*
Potatoes Lyonnaise
Iced lemon mousse

SPRING
April
Avocado vinaigrette
Roast duck with
   cherry sauce *Château la Tour de Cauze 1962 (St Emilion)*
New potatoes with mint and chives
Frozen petit pois
Rhubarb fool

May
Poached trout with herbs *Pouilly Fuissé 1966 (Louis Jadot)*
Sort of Stroganoff *Pommard 1964 (Groffier Léger)*
Creamed potatoes with spring onions
Provençale mushrooms
Chocolate orange mousse

June
Asparagus with Hollandaise sauce *Deidesheimer Siegel 1964*
Lamb chops with butter and herbs *Château Belgrave 1962*
Glazed carrots
Spinach with cream
Summer fruit flan

SUMMER

July
Iced watercress soup
Chilled salmon
    with avocado sauce   *Pouilly Fuissé 1966 (Louis Jadot)*
Potato salad, green salad
Raspberry gâteau

August
Crab cocktail   *Pouilly Blanc Fumé (Grants)*
Chicken Basque style   *Tavel Rosé*
Onion rice, green salad
Brandied plums

September
Kipper pâté
Easy stew 2   } *Nicolas Canteval*
Duchess potatoes
Bilberry cheesecake

AUTUMN

October
Egg Mayonnaise
Veal Marengo   *Margaux (A. Delor & Cie)*
Onion rice
Fruit tart

November
Herring and apple salad
Beef in beer   *Don Cortez Burgundy*
Onion rice and spiced cauliflower
Quick banana dessert

December
Celery soup
Ham in pastry
    with Cumberland sauce   *Châteaneuf du Pape Blanc 1966*
Mashed potato with onion and petit pois
Mincemeat and apple crumble

A selected list of
MAIL ORDER SHOPS

HARRODS LTD, 46 Knightsbridge, London W1.
Specially good for plum cake and Christmas pudding.

SELFRIDGES LTD, Oxford Street, London W1.
Carries large stocks of almost anything in the food line,
including Kosher and Health Foods.

JUSTIN DE BLANC PROVISIONS, 42 Elizabeth Street, London
W1.
Good for homemade jams which you can pretend you
made yourself.

FORTNUM & MASON LTD, 181 Piccadilly, London SW1.
Excellent Dundee cakes that come in tins, if you're thinking
of giving a tea-party. Also lots of posh-sounding but very
expensive teas.

THE HOUSE OF FLORIS, 39 Brewer Street, London W1.
Very special homemade chocolates and excellent iced cele-
bration cakes.

G. PARMIGIANI FIGLIO, 14 Old Compton Street, London W1.
Anything Italian: rice, pastas, whole salamis, very good
canned Bolognese sauce and delicious Italian pickled pimen-
toes. Also tinned white kidney beans (fagioli).

BOMBAY EMPORIUM, 70 Grafton Way, London W1.
Anything you need for curries, including pickles and
chutneys.

MISCELLANEOUS TIPS AND HINTS

The information in this section has been reproduced with the kind permission of the Good Housekeeping Institute.

REFRIGERATOR STORAGE

The following notes should help you to use your refrigerator to best advantage while the Table is intended to give an indication of how long certain foods will keep under refrigeration.

Using a Refrigerator

1. All foods must be covered.

2. Allow hot dishes to cool before storing them, or the ice-making compartment will quickly become covered with frost, and this insulating layer will make it difficult for the air to be satisfactorily cooled.

3. Put in correct part of the refrigerator:
   (a) Raw foods such as meat, bacon, poultry and fish should be kept directly under the frozen food compartment, in the coldest part of the refrigerator.
   (b) Cooked meat, made-up dishes can go on middle shelves.
   (c) Vegetables, salad ingredients and bread go at the bottom, vegetables and salads in the crisper, if any.
   (d) There is usually a compartment inside the door for butter, where it will not become too hard.

4. The 'edge' is taken off the flavour of many foods when they are chilled, so if possible remove such items as cheese, cold meats, salads, sandwiches, etc., from the refrigerator a little while before using them – the time depends on the room temperature. From the cooking angle, eggs and fats should be warmed up before baking time.

5. Wipe up any spilt foods at once, before they harden, and check the contents of the shelves regularly.

6. Defrost the refrigerator regularly, and clean it, using a weak solution of bicarbonate of soda in warm water.

Many refrigerator manufacturers are now labelling the freezer compartment of their refrigerators with a Star Rating, depending on the temperature of the Frozen Food Compartment (*see Table overleaf*).

Maximum Temperature of Frozen Food Compartment	Maximum Storage Time for: (a) Frozen Foods	(b) Ice Cream
*** 0°F	2–3 months	2–3 months
** +10°F	4 weeks	1–2 weeks
* +21°F	1 week	1 day

REFRIGERATOR STORAGE TIMES

Food	How to store	Days
Meat, raw		
Joints	Rinse blood away; wipe dry,	3–5
Chops, cut meat	cover with polythene or foil	2–4
Minced meat, offal	Cover as above	1–2
Sausages	Cover as above	3
Bacon	Wrap in foil or polythene, or put in plastic container	7
Meat, cooked		
Joints	In tightly wrapped foil or poly-	3–5
Sliced ham	thene, or in lidded container	2–3
Continental sausages	In tightly wrapped foil or poly- thene, or in lidded container	3–5
Casseroles	In tightly wrapped foil or poly- thene, or in lidded container	2–3
Poultry, raw		
Whole or joints	Draw, wash, wipe dry. Wrap in polythene or foil	2–3
Poultry, cooked		
Whole or joints	Remove stuffing; when cool, wrap or cover as for cooked meats	2–3
Made-up dishes	Cover when cool	1
Fish, raw (white, oily, smoked)	Cover loosely in foil or polythene	1–2
Fish, cooked	As above, or in covered container	2
Shellfish	Eat the day it is bought – don't store	

Food	How to store	Days
Vegetables, salads		
Prepared green and root vegetables, green beans, celery, courgettes, aubergines, peppers	In crisper drawer, or in plastic container, or wrapped in polythene	5–8
Sweet corn, mushrooms, tomatoes, radishes, spring onions	Clean or wipe as necessary; store in covered container	5–7
Lettuce, cucumber, cut onions, cut peppers, parsley	Clean or wipe as necessary; store in covered container	4 6
Cress, watercress	Clean or wipe as necessary; store in covered container	2
Fresh fruit		
Cut oranges, grapefruit, lemons	In covered container	3–4
Strawberries, redcurrants, raspberries, peaches	In covered container	1–3
Grapes, cherries, gooseberries, cut melon	In covered container	5–7
Rhubarb, cleaned	In covered container	6–10
Eggs		
Fresh, in shell	In rack, pointed end down	14
Yolks	In lidded plastic container	2–3
Whites	In lidded plastic container	3–4
Hard boiled, in shell	Uncovered	up to 7
Fats		
Butter, margarine	In original wrapper, in special compartment of refrigerator	14–21
Cooking fats	In original wrapper, in special compartment of refrigerator	28

Food	How to store	Days
Milk, etc		
Milk	In original container, closed	3–4
Cream	In original container, closed	2–4
Soured cream, buttermilk, yogurt	In original container, closed	7
Milk sweets, custards	Lightly covered with foil or film	2
Cheese		
Parmesan, in piece	In film, foil or airtight container	21–28

STORAGE IN A LARDER OR STORE-CUPBOARD

A larder, if cool and ventilated, gives the next best storage after a refrigerator – in fact, for some foods it's preferable – but many homes nowadays have only non-ventilated food storage cupboards, which are of more limited usefulness.

The following notes are intended as helpful guidelines to larder and store-cupboard storage while the Table is intended as a handy reference to the keeping qualities of the different kinds of foodstuffs stored:

1. All food stored in larder or cupboard should be kept in covered containers or suitable wrappings. Containers with closely fitting lids are recommended for non-perishable foods, especially those of a granular or powdery texture, which clog in moist conditions. Airtight containers are essential for commodities whose flavour is vital, such as coffee and spices, and for crisp-textured biscuits, etc.

2. Foods for long-term larder storage should be placed on the higher or less accessible shelves, while perishables and regularly-used foods should be close at hand. Use foods in the order in which they were bought, putting new purchases at the back of the shelves.

3. Food bought in packets, e.g., flour, sugar may be stored in that way until opened; then the contents should be transferred to airtight containers. Labelling is important, especially when the foods look alike.

4. Quick-dried foods, such as peas, packet soups, and some packaged foods, deteriorate when exposed to air, heat and moisture, but may be stored satisfactorily in the unopened packet or airtight jar if kept in a dry, cool place.

5. Canned foods should have the date of purchase marked on the label and should be used in rotation. Discard any 'blown' can, shown by bulged ends and leaking seams. If, however, you see a cheap buy in a dented can, this is safe, provided there is no sign of rust or seepage from the seams, but use up such cans quickly.

6. Most canned foods are perfectly sound for periods longer than given in the chart, but excessively long storage may mean that flavour and texture are not so good.

7. Don't store dog and cat cereals, biscuits, etc. in the larder — any infestation that might be present could spread rapidly to other commodities. (If this should happen, all affected food-stuff must be destroyed and the container washed, sterilised and well dried before re-use.)

LARDER AND FOOD-CUPBOARD STORAGE TIMES

Notes: Times refer to unopened packets, jars or cans. Perishables such as fish, meat, poultry, milk, cream, should be stored for only about 1 day, covered as for refrigerator storage.

Food	Keeping qualities, time	Storage comments
Flour, white	Up to 6 months	Once opened, transfer
Wheatmeal	Up to 3 months	to container with
Wholemeal	Up to 1 month	close-fitting lid
Baking powder, bicarbonate of soda, cream of tartar	2–3 months	Dry storage essential; if opened, put in container with close-fitting lid
Dried yeast	Up to 6 months	As above
Cornflour, custard powder	Good keeping qualities	As above
Pasta	As above	As above
Rice, all types	As above	As above

Food	Keeping qualities, time	Storage comments
Sugar, loaf, caster, granulated	As above	Cool, dry storage; if opened, transfer as above
Sugar, icing, brown	Limited life – tends to absorb moisture	Buy in small quantities, as required
Tea	Limited life – loses flavour if stored long	Buy in small quantities; store in airtight container in dry, cool place
Instant and ground coffee in sealed can or jar	Up to 1 year	Cool, dry storage; once opened, re-seal securely; use quickly
Coffee beans, loose ground coffee	Very limited life; use immediately	Buy as required; use airtight container
Instant low-fat skimmed milk	3 months	Cool, dry storage is vital; once opened, re-seal securely; use fairly quickly
Breakfast cereals	Limited life	Buy in small quantities. Cool, dry place
Dehydrated foods	Up to 1 year	Cool, dry place. If opened, fold packet down tightly and use within a week
Herbs, spices, seasonings	6 months	Cool, dry storage, in airtight container. Keep from light. Buy in small quantities
Nuts, ground almonds, desiccated coconut	Limited life – depends on freshness when bought. Fat content goes rancid if kept too long	Lidded container

Food	Keeping qualities, time	Storage comments
Dried fruits	2–3 months	Cool, dry storage
Jams, etc.	Good keeping quality	Dry, cool, dark storage
Honey, clear or thick	As above	Dry, cool storage. After about 1 year, appearance may alter, but honey is still fit to eat
Golden syrup, treacle	As above	As above
Condensed milk	4–6 months	Safe even after some years, but caramelises and thickens. Once opened, harmless crust forms; cover can with foil lid and use within 1 month
Evaporated milk	6–8 months	Safe even after some years, but darkens, thickens and loses flavour. Once opened, treat as fresh milk
Canned fruit	12 months	Cool, dry place
Canned vegetables	2 years	Cool, dry place
Canned fish in oil	Up to 5 years	Cool, dry place
Canned fish in tomato sauce	Up to 1 year	Cool, dry place
Canned meat	Up to 5 years	As above. Cans holding 1 kilo or more should be kept in refrigerator
Canned ham	6 months	

Food	Keeping qualities, time	Storage comments
Pickles, sauces	Reasonably good keeping qualities	Cool, dry, dark place
Chutneys	Limited life	As above
Vinegars	Good keeping qualities – at least up to 2 years	Cool, dry, dark place; strong light affects flavoured vinegar and produces a non-bacterial cloudiness. Re-seal after use; never return unused vinegar to bottle
Oils (olive, corn)	Up to 18 months	Cool, dry place

FOODS IN SEASON

Fruit

Apples, Bananas, Grapes, Grapefruit, Pears, Pineapple, Melons, Oranges: *all year round*

Apricots: *May–August; December–February*

Avocados: *October–April*

Blackberries: *July–October*

Blackcurrants: *June–August*

Cherries: *June–August*

Chestnuts: *December–February*

Cranberries: *November–January*

Damsons: *August–October*

Figs: *September–December*

Gooseberries: *July–September*

Mandarins: *November–February; December–March*

Nectarines: *July–October*

Peaches: *January–October*

Plums: *December–October*

Raspberries: *May–August*

Strawberries: *January–August*

Rhubarb (not strictly a fruit): *December–June*

Game and Wild Birds

Black Game: *August 20–December 12*

Duck (wild): *August 1–March 1*

Grouse: *August 12–December 12*

Hare: *August 1–February 28*

Partridge: *September 1–February 8*

Pheasant: *October 1–February 1*

Plover:
  October 1–March 15
Ptarmigan:
  August 12–December 12
Quail: *All year*
Rabbit:
  September 1–April 30
Snipe:
  October 1–March 1
Teal:
  October–February
Venison:
  July 1–February 28
Widgeon:
  October–February
Woodcock:
  August 1–March 1
Wood Pigeon:
  August 1– March 15

Fish and Shellfish

Cod: *All year*
Dab: *All year*
Halibut: *All year*
Herrings: *All year*
Mackerel: *All year*
Crab: *All year*
Lobster: *All year*
Oysters : *September–April*
Plaice: *All year*
Salmon: *February–August*
Sole: *All year*
Trout: *March–August*
Turbot: *All year*
Prawns: *All year*
Scallops: *November–March*
Shrimps: *All year*

Poultry

Capon: *All year*

Chicken: *All year*
Poussin: *All year*
Duck: *March–September*
Goose: *September–February*
Guinea Fowl: *All year*
Pigeon: *All year*
Turkey: *September–March*

Vegetables, Salads

Aubergines, Beetroot, Cabbage,
Carrots, Onions, Potatoes, Tur-
nips, Mushrooms, Spinach: *all
the year round.*
Artichokes, Globe:
  March–November
    Jerusalem: *March–July*
Asparagus: *April–July*
Beans, French
  February–March
    Broad: *April–July*
    Runner: *June–September*
Broccoli: *October–April*
Brussels Sprouts:
  September–March
Cauliflower: *June–March*
Celery: *August–February,
  April–May*
Celeriac: *September–March*
Courgettes: *June–September*
Leeks: *September–April*
Parsnips: *September–April*
Peas: *May– October*
New Potatoes:
  May–September
Lettuce (round), Endive, Cu-
cumber, Watercress, Capsicums
(peppers), Tomatoes, Radish:
all the year round. Webb and
Cos Lettuce: *available during
summer months*

LARGE SCALE CATERING

General Calculations (Per head)

Cocktail party: 4 or 5 small savouries and 3 or 4 drinks.

Fork buffet: 1 starter, 1 main dish, 1 sweet, 3 or 4 drinks.

Wedding reception: 4–6 savouries, 1–2 sweet foods, 3–4 drinks.

Adult tea-party: 3–4 savoury items, 2 small cakes or slices of cake, 2 cups of tea.

Teenage party: 1 main dish, plenty of crusty bread, butter, cheese, 1 sweet dish, 4–6 drinks (coffee and cold soft drinks in variety).

Children's party (for the under-tens): 4–6 savoury items, including potato crisps, cheesy biscuits, baby sausages; 1–2 sweet items, of which ice cream is certainly one; and 2 cold drinks (milk and fruit squash).

Sandwich Fillings

Each filling is sufficient for 12 rounds using a 2-lb. loaf and 6 oz. butter, or about 12 small bridge rolls split in half and topped with the filling.

8 eggs, hard-boiled and mashed, or scrambled.

14–16 oz. cold meat, sliced or minced and seasoned.

2 7 oz. cans of salmon (mashed, seasoned and suitably garnished).

4 4¾ oz. cans of sardines (as above).

2 7 oz. cans of tuna (as above).

12 oz. Cheddar or other hard cheese, finely grated and softened with butter or mayonnaise.

6–8 oz. cream or cottage cheese, seasoned or with chopped chives added.

4 bananas, mashed, with a little lemon juice, and chopped walnuts or dates added to taste.

Note. An even and economical way to spread butter on bread is to start at the corners and spread inwards – not to slap a large lump in the middle and try to work it to the corners.

FRYING TEMPERATURES

(oil or fat for deep frying)

If you have no thermometer, judge the heat by the time taken to brown a 1-inch cube of bread.

Doughnuts, fritters, onions, uncooked fish
350–360°F   60 seconds
Croquettes, cooked food
360–380°F   40 seconds
Potato chips, crisps, straws
370–390°F   20 seconds

OVEN TEMPERATURES

Oven	°F	°C	Gas Mark
Very cool	250–275	121–135	¼–½
Cool	300	149	1–2
Warm	325	163	3
Moderate	350	177	4
Fairly hot	375–400	190–204	5–6
Hot	425	218	7
Very hot	450–475	232–246	8–9

NB. To convert Centigrade temperatures to Fahrenheit, multiply by 9, divide by 5 and then add 32. Conversely, to turn a Fahrenheit temperature into Centigrade, subtract 32, multiply by 5 and divide by 9.

HANDY MEASURES

		Approx.
Almonds, ground	1 oz. = 3¾	level tbsps
Breadcrumbs, fresh	1 oz. = 7	„ „
dried	1 oz. = 3¼	„ „
Butter, lard, etc,	1 oz. = 2	„ „
Cheese, Cheddar grated	1 oz. = 3	„ „
Chocolate, grated	1 oz. = 3¼	„ „
Cocoa	1 oz. = 2¾	„ „
Coconut, desiccated	1 oz. = 5	„ „
Coffee, instant	1 oz. = 6½	„ „
Coffee, ground	1 oz. = 4	„ „
Cornflour, custard powder	1 oz. = 2½	„ „
Curry powder	1 oz. = 5	„ „
Flour, unsifted	1 oz. = 3	„ „

		Approx.
Gelatine, powdered	1 oz. = 2½	level tbsps
Ginger, ground	1 oz. = 4½	„ „
Mustard, dry	1 oz. = 3½	„ „
Rice, uncooked	1 oz. = 1½	„ „
Sugar, granulated, caster	1 oz. = 2	„ „
icing	1 oz. = 2½	„ „
Syrup, unheated	1 oz. = 1	„ „
Yeast, granulated	1 oz. = 1½	„ „

Liquid ingredients—water, milk, corn oil

2 tablespoonfuls = 1¼ fl. oz. = $\frac{1}{16}$ pint
4 „ = 2½ „ = $\frac{1}{8}$ „
6 „ = 3¾ „ = $\frac{3}{16}$ „
8 „ = 5 „ = $\frac{1}{4}$ „

COMPARATIVE MEASURES

American cup (8 fl. oz. capacity)	Weight in ounces Approximate	Weight in grams Approximate
Butter, margarine, lard	8	227
Suet, shredded	4	120
Cheddar cheese, grated	4	113
Cream, double	8	236
Milk, condensed	11	306
Milk, evaporated	9	255
Breadcrumbs – fresh	1	28
Rice	6½	182
Flour – plain, self-raising	4	113
Currants	5	142
Raisins – seedless	6	164
Raisins – stoned	5	142
Dates, stoned, and chopped peel	6	178
Cherries, glacé	7	198
Almonds, whole and blanched	6	152
Walnuts, halved	4	100
Sugar – granulated, caster	7	198
Sugar – icing	4½	128
Syrups and honey	11½	328

METRIC CONVERSIONS

If you want to convert recipes from imperial to metric, we recommend that you use 25 grammes as a basic unit in place of 1 oz., 500 ml in place of 1 pint, and take the new British Standard 5-ml and 15-ml spoons in place of the old variable teaspoons and tablespoons; these adaptations will give a slightly smaller recipe quantity.

For more exact conversions and general reference, the following tables will be helpful:

Mass (Weight)

g=gramme; kg=kilogramme

1 oz.	= 28.35 g	2 lb.=907 g	
4 oz. (¼ lb.)	=113 g	3 lb.=1.36 kg	
8 oz. (½ lb.)	=227 g	4 lb.=1.81 kg	
16 oz. (1 lb.)	=454 g	5 lb.=2.27 kg	
1½ lb.	=681 g	10 lb.=4.54 kg	

Capacity

ml=millilitre; l=litre

¼ pint =142 ml	1¾ pints=994 ml		
½ pint =284 ml	2 pints=1.14 l		
¾ pint =426 ml	2½ pints=1.42 l		
1 pint =568 ml	3 pints=1.70 l		
1¼ pints=710 ml	3½ pints=1.99 l		
1½ pints=852 ml			

Length

cm=centimetre

1 inch=2.54 cm	1 foot=30.48 cm

Temperatures

Fahrenheit	Celsius	Fahrenheit	Celsius
32°F (water freezes) = 0°C		325°F	=163°C
205°F (simmering) = 96°C		350°F	=177°C
212°F (water boils) =100°C		375°F	=190°C
225°F =107°C		400°F	=204°C
250°F =121°C		425°F	=218°C
275°F =135°C		450°F	=232°C
300°F =149°C			

Note: Centigrade is another name for the Celsius scale.

Energy

The basic unit used in calculating energy in nutrition is the Calorie (Kilocalorie), but it is probable that when the S.I. (Système International or International System) metric units are adopted in the U.K., the unit of energy known as the *joule* will be adopted. The equivalent value is as follows: 1 Calorie (Kilocalorie)=4.19 Kilojoules.

INDEX

INDEX